So Much Blood

And Other Stories from the Potato Field

Edgar (Ted) Stubbersfield (Editor)

Matt 13:[3]"A farmer went out to sow his seed. [4] As he was scattering the seed, ... seed fell on good soil, where it produced a crop—a hundred, sixty or thirty times what was sown. [9] Whoever has ears, let them hear."

ISBN: 0-9944157-7-X
ISBN-13: 978-0-9944157-7-6

CONTENTS

Acknowledgments   i

Introduction   Pg. 1

1   Follow Me and I Will Give You That Farm   Pg. 3

2   It's In The Good Lord's Hands Now   Pg. 8

3   A Gideon Bible Saved A Life   Pg. 10

4   So Much Blood   Pg. 15

5   God's Leading and Provision   Pg. 17

6   Am I Not able to Take Care of You   Pg. 26

7   Transition to Retirement   Pg. 36

8   The Crooked Made Straight   Pg. 38

9   The Healing Power of Forgiveness   Pg. 41

10   The Ups and Downs of a Boy From the   Pg. 47

11   The Engine Just Stopped   Pg. 55

12   The Engine Stopped Again   Pg. 57

13   Watched Over by Angels   Pg. 59

14   Pray for Your Husband   Pg. 62

15   It Rained for 40 days and 40 nights   Pg.63

16   I Thank God for my Husband   Pg. 66

17   Nine Months Turned into Nine Years   Pg. 69

18   Stanley Wasn't Ready for Heaven   Pg. 73

19   We are not Done Yet   Pg. 76

20   Great is Thy Faithfulness   Pg. 81

21	Giving Thanks	Pg 84
22	Restoration in the Potato Field	Pg 88
23	A Call to Missions	Pg 95
24	God is Provider	Pg 99
25	The Best Day of My Life	Pg 110
26	One of a Kind	Pg 113
27	God's Grace for Healing	Pg 115
28	Reserved	Pg 117
29	Getting off the Tightrope	Pg 120
30	Called to Walk Together	Pg 125
31	The Lord Stopped a Bolting Horse	Pg 124
30	A Friend of Mine	Pg 126
	About the Editor	Pg 129

ACKNOWLEDGMENTS

I would like to thank those members, past and present of Tenthill Baptist Church, who shared their stories of faith with me. There are many more, of course, that have not been told and it will not be until we meet the Good Lord face to face that we will know the full extent of his goodness towards us. It is hoped that this book's final chapter has not been written and more stories of faith will be added

.

INTRODUCTION

When I first started to study theology, there was a deep divide among the student body. One side was very adamant that the age of miracles had passed with the death of the apostles while the other side believed that we could ask for the Lord's help today in the most dire of circumstances. The divide was often between those with theology but little experience and those with little theology but having an experience. Often there was not much love in the dispute nor much clarity of thought for surely a God who is entirely passive and always unavailable is, for all practical purposes, non-existent.[1]

About 300 years after the deaths of the apostles, when miracles were said to have ceased, the great theologian, Augustine, Bishop of Hippo in North Africa also died. When I read what he had to say about miracles in his book *The City of God*, I marvelled at his accounts of what occurred, in and around his diocese. His flock actively proclaimed their experiences through stories which were kept and publicly read. In two years, over 70 miracles were recorded at one location alone in Hippo!

Over the years I also have heard wonderful testimonies of the Lord's salvation and provision but they are almost all lost now. This little book is an attempt to show the journey of faith of people who, at one stage or presently, call the little chapel in the potato patch their home. It is hoped that by recording them, at least some of these stories will remain to be pondered by the next generation.

There is no unifying theme among the accounts, I have just asked, "Tell me of a time when the Good Lord drew near and made his presence felt." For some, this time is at their conversion while for

---

[1] Anderson, R. *The Silence of God.* (Pickering & Inglis: London, 9th edition) 10.

others it is in a lifetime walked close to Jesus. For others, still it was help in a time of crisis. On reading these stories of faith you may be tempted to think that the Tenthill Baptists are different to other people but nothing could be further from the truth. We experience the same joys and know the same sufferings and trials as our unbelieving neighbours. But there is a difference in that we, like all disciples of Jesus, do not walk them alone. We have learned that our heavenly Father is not always busy elsewhere.

While these tales often record the extraordinary, each story teller would want you see a loving and gracious Heavenly Father in his daily leading and provision. Perhaps, in this, Augustine can have the last word:

"For he that made from five loaves bread to fill so many thousands was the same who daily prepares mighty harvests in the earth from but a few grains. For this too is a miracle of God, Although we have ceased to wonder at it because it comes about day by day"[2]

May you be blessed to encounter the Good Lord in the day to day living of your life and also be blessed to know the extraordinary.

Ted Stubbersfield
18 May 2018

---

[2]E. & M-L Keller *Miracles in Dispute* (Dallas: Probe 1982). P.25 Quoting Augustine *Enarrationes in Psalmos* XC; Sermones1,i.

1. FOLLOW ME AND I WILL GIVE YOU THAT FARM

This is the testimony of Reg Crust, an elder in the Tent hill church for many years. He tells of his conversion and the Lord's promise of second potato farm and his intention to bless many through it. Reg was born in 1934.

I left my parents' home in Wynnum at the age of 21 to come to Tent Hill where I worked on the Garmeister farm, living with them till 1959. My first introduction to the gospel was, each night, hearing Mrs. Garmeister give devotions to her two sons Barry and Neville.[3] Heather Jackwitz, who I would marry in 1960, lived across the road where her parents also were farmers. We moved back to Wynnum where we lived with my parents for six months. During this time we purchased a parcel delivery service and built

---

3 The Garmeister farm surrounds the church in the potato field.

the business up allowing us to purchase our own home in Wynnum

The father of Keith Dorr (Heather's sister Joan's husband) died and, sitting around the table in Wynnum, I saw that he was in trouble. We shook hands and I decided to go to Mt Sylvia[4] to help Keith on the farm. We did not discuss this with our wives! By this stage Heather and I had three children and a fourth was on the way. We were able to sell the business in just two weeks and moved to a new home on the Dorr farm. For two years our lives and that of the Dorr's intertwined. During this time I was saved from death twice, once in an incident involving powerlines, an irrigation pipe and wet grass, the other at flooded pipes at a creek crossing.

Heather and I purchased a farm at My Sylvia in 1967. We were heavily in debt with both the farm and the Wynnum home and success with the first crop was essential. During the five years that it took to pay off the farm I came to understand that we were not alone.

In 1973 I was out in the farm shifting irrigation pipes near the house and looking out across from the next farm I saw my neighbour, Rex Kleinschmidt, a Lutheran. The farm was on the market and I said in my mind, "Lord, that farm should be mine". Just then I heard a voice shouting from behind, "If you give your life to me the farm is yours." It affected me profoundly but I told no one. That weekend an evangelist came to the church for a campaign termed, *Alive and Free in 73*. I did not respond but my daughter Cheryl asked if we could have the speaker for lunch but I deflected the question by saying, "Ask your mother".

No one had ever asked me if I was a Christian, everyone just thought I was but I certainly was not a believer. I had gone to church with Heather to keep harmony and could never understand

---

4 Situated further up one of the valleys from Tent Hill.

why people went to the front of the church and ask for prayer after a call to give your life to Christ. The evangelist said over dinner table, "Reg, you are not a Christian, you had better do something about it, look at your family, you must do something about it, you need to be honourable to your family in being up front". Then he said no more. On leaving he invited me to the service in Gatton that night. "Maybe," I replied but I felt compelled to go. There was an alter call and his voice from the farm haunted me again but I could not get up. Despite only being 39 I felt like an old man and Heather had to help me stand. I wobbled down the aisle and saw Pastor Ralph Cameron. Heather let me go and I went straight to Ralph who said, "Reg, the Lord is dealing with you isn't he". "Yes Pastor Cameron" and in tears I prayed a prayer of repentance.

Back on the farm the next day I was shifting irrigation pipes in the potato patch and my neighbour was also out shifting pipes. We met at the road and I told him about giving my life to the Lord. I went on to say "Your farm that you are selling, the Lord says it is going to be mine. But I can't afford to buy it but the Lord says it will be mine". Rex was desperate to sell his farm but, despite that, he went into Gatton and took it off all the agents. Two days later he came back and told me, "I am waiting for you to buy the farm". "I can't afford it," I said, but he replied, "I'll wait".

Next year I had another crop of potatoes and Rex was counting the loads coming off my farm. He knew the prices and he came over and said, "Now you have the money to buy the farm." I rang the bank manager and told him how much I needed, "you have it to the dollar, come in to the bank in the morning and we will make out the cheque and buy the farm." The crop of 1974 was very heavy and the prices were good and we knew more funds were coming in. We have never had a crop like it since!

I was baptised in April 1973, two weeks later and my baptismal verse was Galatians 2:20 "I have been crucified with Christ and I no longer live, but Christ lives in me. The life I now live in the body, I live by faith in the Son of God, who loved me and gave himself for me."

We did not know what to do with the home on the new farm so we started to ask what we should do with it. In mid-1976 the Anglican Church in Gatton, which then had a strong young people's group, asked to use it for a camp, a use far removed from our mind. They came again with a different age group and again, three camps in a row. They told us that this place had so much potential for a camp. We spoke to Pastor Cameron who believed this was right and we prayed about the matter. Then the Baptist Union advised what we should do – not to charge for a camp "even though people will use you and take you for a ride." We advertised in the Baptist magazine and we had 48 camps for the rest of the year. I do not know how we found time for potatoes and the camp. The camp may have had minimal facilities but despite this four people came to faith in the first year. The camp proved a training ground for the younger members of the church and many were saved there as well.

The local council was helpful, amazing as at that time they were obstructive on other matters. The facilities were upgraded with an ablution block which "put a shine on the place." We were able to have bookings for 85-95% of the year just by word of mouth. Public liability issues and the need to have $80 million insurance cover saw the camp close in 2001 after 24 years. The insurers could not cope with walking on the mountain, large playing fields and the flying fox but these were what the campers loved, along with the clear stars at night. In that time the Solomon Island ministry who regularly used the camp became very close to our heart.

In my church life I served as a deacon, secretary, elder and also worked with the South Sea Evangelical Mission. Heather has being doing Religious Instruction (RI) in Schools for 40 years and ran RI camps every October with 50-70 children attending and saw many give their lives to Jesus. She was also a church function speaker for Scripture Union At home we had several exchange students from overseas. We were always given the trouble makers who proved to be no trouble at all.

We retired in 2014 and moved to Gatton. We gave one farm to our son Brian and sold the second farm to him as well as now he needed more land to be viable.

"To God be the glory great things he hath done." Many people had their lives transformed even our family. "Praise God".

2. IT IS IN THE GOOD LORD'S HANDS NOW

This is the testimony of Rachel Stubbersfield, the wife of the editor of this book. She was diagnosed with very aggressive breast cancer in 1988.

Late in October 1988, the routine removal of a lump in Rachel's left breast uncovered a very aggressive type of cancer. A mastectomy was performed the next day and we were then told the cancer had spread under Rachel's breast bone. A further operation was performed to remove the lymph nodes under her arm, four of which had turned cancerous. The surgeon advised 'two years you would be doing well, three would be most exceptional' Her death would be painful. With all hope gone I could only answer "it is obviously in the Good Lord's hand's now and I suppose when you think about it, there is no better place for it to be". The Surgeon agreed, while the anaesthetist consoled me with the hope we have in heaven. The pathologist's report came back a few days later. There was no sign of the cancer in the lymph nodes seen by the surgeon and anaesthetist, causing the surgeon to revise his prognosis.

We still would not presume upon the Lord's mercy and believed chemotherapy and radiation still to be prudent.

Rachel had experienced a ' special peace' in her life some weeks before the diagnosis and this helped her through the trials and gave her an unshakable trust in the Lord. She even ministered to the hospital chaplain! My faith on the other hand was dealt a blow. A spirit of prayer came over Gatton for Rachel. There was not a church in Gatton where fervent prayers were not held for her healing. The heavens opened when the Lutheran pastor blessed Rachel while making the sign of the cross on her forehead. The pastor of the Baptist church would pray publicly in tears. We were participants of something that came deep from the heart of God.

Two years later I said to our surgeon, "It looks as if God has been very merciful to us". "The Lord works in mysterious way's His wonders to perform" was his reply and this was from a man who, at that time, had treated 2000 cases or more of breast cancer. I know that what we received at the Lord's hand was extraordinary and that for many the path is through pain and suffering with "only" His grace and the love of the family to sustain them. For ourselves we know not to look within for a reason for God's mercy. Almost 30 years later there is no sign of the cancer.

3. A GIDEON BIBLE SAVED A LIFE

At the time of writing Greg Sharpe is an Elder at Tenthill Baptist Church and the president of the Lockyer camp of Gideons International. This testimony in his own words tells the remarkable outcome from a normal visit to a motel to check the Bibles. The names are changed.

"He demanded that the Bibles be removed and destroyed!" Linda exclaimed.

Linda had enthusiastically agreed to the Bibles being placed in their motel so she refused to meet Allan's demand which was one of many domineering demands he was making on her life. Linda and Allan were business and personal partners. The motel was business and home and they were in financial debt so Linda had no means of escape from the demands.

Linda and Allan had moved from interstate, about a year earlier, to their new business venture; a small motel in a small country town, South East Queensland, Linda left behind two sons from a previous relationship and, to her dismay, Allan strove to make it impossible for her to continue contact with them.

Linda had also left behind contact with a Church congregation; to her despair, management of the motel prevented her from establishing contact with any Church congregation in their new community. The role restrained Linda to the motel seven days a week as Allan was also conducting another business and therefore didn't relieve her of the workload. On many Sunday mornings Linda peered out from the motel as if imprisoned and yearned to join the congregation that she watched entering a nearby Church; when she expressed her desire to Allan he insisted that ... HE WOULD BE HER GOD.

Linda began to believe that Allan's motive for the move to the motel was to gain total control over her life. She became fearful as Allan proclaimed such love for her that ... HE WANTED TO BE BURIED WITH HER. After Allan deliberately drove dangerously while she was a passenger in his work ute[5] she perceived that she was living under a veil of threat against her life.

The domineering demands continued until Allan expelled Linda from the motel leaving her without home and money. She had no option but to move into a home adjacent to the highway not far from town. It was not long before Allan requested Linda's return to the motel but she refused as she feared the threat against her life. It was only a few days later, in the early hours of the morning, that there was much commotion on the highway at the entrance to the property where she was staying. Linda saw the ambulances and police but it was several hours before she learned that Allan had deliberately driven into an oncoming truck and was killed instantly; his work ute was destroyed beyond recognition. It remains a mystery how he timed the high speed collision to occur at the entrance to the property where Linda was staying.

Despite the veil of threat over Linda's life she was preserved; but this is not the end of the story because there it is another perspective that is relevant to each one of us.

---

5 Short for utility vehicle. Utes are Australian icons deriving from 1933 when a Gippsland farmer's wife wrote a letter to Ford Australia, asking: "Can you build me a vehicle that we can use to go to church in on Sunday, without getting wet, and that my husband can use to take the pigs to market on Monday?"

The placement of Bibles in the motel was intended for the benefit of the motel patrons but it played a part in preserving the life of the motel manager.

During October 2016 my wife, Anne, and I were returning home, on a Monday morning, after a weekend away. We had enough Bibles with us to place in a small motel, on behalf of The Gideons International. As we passed through a small country town we stopped at the first motel we saw. Strangely, the manager could not be found so we moved to the next motel where I found the manageress, Linda, at the reception desk.

Linda immediately noticed the Bible that I was carrying and welcomed me; she had been yearning for contact with a Church congregation and here was an apparent representative stepping into the place of her imprisonment! She was so enthusiastic that after I explained the purpose of my visit she immediately agreed to the placement of the Bibles and accompanied me from room to room. To be accompanied by the motel manager was unusual but even more so because Linda expressed more of her personal life as we progressed from room to room. By the time we returned to reception she was becoming emotional so I suggested that my wife, who was waiting in the car, join us. After Anne came in, Linda described the threatening veil that she was living under. She was grateful when we prayed for her welfare in the very place where she felt alone, threatened and imprisoned. A few months later, after Allan's death, Linda told us that not a day had passed without her recalling our visit. Neither Anne nor I could have comprehended the impact of our visit or the part it would play in the preservation of Linda's life.

God's Word proclaims "For we are His workmanship, created in Christ Jesus for good works, which God prepared beforehand so that we would walk in them". **Eph. 2:10**

God graciously prepared, beforehand, our visit to Linda by having us in the right place at the right time so that we could be a blessing to her. This is a reminder that our part is to be available to follow the ministry that God has called us to. For Anne and I, God's call is to the ministry of The Gideons International but this reminder is relevant to each of us. Check your calling and availability!

At the conclusion of our visit Linda agreed to a visit from a Pastor. Although Pastor Gary was in a neighbouring town he was the only Pastor I knew who was close enough to visit Linda; I had met him only a few months before through the Gideon ministry. After informing Pastor Gary of Linda's state of despair he not only visited her but later arranged contact between her and the nearby Church congregation that she had watched from her window many Sunday mornings. Women from that congregation, including the Pastor's wife, provided Linda with the support that she had desired and they too began to pray for her.

To protect the privacy of the motel manageress the names I have used, except Anne, are pseudonyms and I have not named the town.

After Allan's death, early 2017, Pastor Gary informed me of what had transpired since October 2016. His report prompted Anne and I to visit Linda a second time. During our second visit Linda agreed that her life had been preserved through God's answer to prayers during and since our first visit; otherwise, a similar collision might have led to two deaths.

Prayer is the aspect of this account that is especially relevant to each one of us.

Other members of our Association were praying for the proposed Bible placement on that Monday morning during October 2016. Being a small motel in a small town it might have seemed insignificant by comparison with some of the other Bible placements we do but nevertheless they prayed. God's Gracious answer to prayer extended well beyond our petitions.

The evil presence that we encountered, indirectly, in October 2016 reminded me that when God's Word is being placed, presented or proclaimed we must:

" ... With all prayer and petition pray at all times in the Spirit, and with this in view, be on the alert with all perseverance and petition for all the saints ..." **Eph. 6v18**; because:

"... our struggle is not against flesh and blood, but against the rulers, against the powers, against the world forces of this

darkness, against the spiritual forces of wickedness in the heavenly places." **Eph. 6v12**

To God by the glory for His Gracious leading and intervention!

4. SO MUCH BLOOD

This testimony is from John Lamb a former Elder in our church John was a very respected GP in Gatton. It tells of his involvement in the aftermath of a violent attack that shook the whole community, not just the community of faith. John said that he had never seen so much blood in all his life. The tragedy is that the people attacked, friends of many at Tenthill, had been previously trying to help the perpetrator.

During my time as a member of Tenthill Baptist Church, I was privileged to meet with other Christians in the area to pray that people in our area would come to know Jesus as their Lord and Saviour.

Very late one night I received a phone call from one of these prayer warriors asking that I pray for him and his family, as they had just been attacked in their beds with a knife by an intruder, They had been woken by being stabbed in the neck and chest. The intruder, a person known to them, had fled. I immediately drove to their house, and arrived at the same time as the police and ambulance. The injuries were serious, verging on critical, however they eventually recovered.

Their children were asleep in their own beds, and were unharmed. After he was arrested by police, the attacker said that he intended to kill the whole family, including the children, but that although he had gone to the children's bedroom first he had not been able to find them.

I believe that God had miraculously kept the children hidden from this man, even though they were in their beds. I also believe that God had protected my friends from fatal injuries.

5. GOD'S LEADING AND PROVISION

Peter Smith was pastor at Tenthill Baptist Church for eleven years concluding in 2003. This story of faith recounts how God has led and provided for both he and his wife Rae

At the age of twenty years, while serving in the Royal Australian Air Force (RAAF) at Wagga Wagga in New South Wales (NSW), Christ brought me to Himself. I started to attend the Church of Christ in town. One of the RAAF fellows who attended there invited me to the Bible study on our RAAF base. I went along and was impressed by this group of airmen and airwomen. The peace and joy that they displayed attracted me. One day I remember walking past the base picture theatre on my way back to my barracks, and thinking I must read the Bible to see what it said. I had owned Bibles for years but had hardly ever read it. So, over the next few months, I read it until I saw that I was a sinner who needed a Saviour. Assurance of salvation was given to me and I sought to live for Christ. I was able to influence a few fellows for Christ. Right from the start, there was a conviction that the Lord wanted me to become a missionary.

After my time in Wagga I was transferred to Laverton, near Melbourne, Victoria, to do training as a radio technician. Once I had graduated I was posted to Williamtown, just outside of Newcastle in NSW.

It was at this time that I read C.T. Studd's life story ("C.T. Studd, Cricketer and Pioneer" by Norman Grubb) and was quite impressed. CT eventually founded the Worldwide Evangelisation Crusade (WEC). While based in Laverton I had attended a WEC meeting and heard of their Missionary Training College (MTC) in Tasmania

During the time I was at Williamtown I felt that it was God's time for me to go to the MTC in Launceston. I applied for a discharge and my Flight-Sargent told me I would never get it. My Flight-Lieutenant told me that it was highly unlikely. Of my six years stint I had signed up for I had only done three and a half years. Also I had not given the three months' notice (before MTC started) required to process my discharge. I wavered between confidence and doubt. Just two weeks, exactly, before the start of the college course, my Flight-Lieutenant called me in to his office and told me that I would be discharged in a week's time. What a miraculous answer to prayer! I arrived at MTC just a day or two before lectures started after three days on the road and overnight on the sea crossing.

In my second year at MTC lots of people in my intake were announcing where the Lord had called them to. So, as the year progressed, I started to get a bit concerned about not knowing. I decided to sign out for lunch once a week to pray and fast. (We were allowed to sign out for two lunch meals a week.) I prayed and fasted for a number of lunchtimes still not knowing. Indonesia had been an interest of mine for some time but I had no certainty on it. On one day of prayer, after communal prayer times in the morning, I went off to pray by myself down at the North Esk River that borders the college property. Stewart Dinnen, the principal, had talked about fully surrendering to God's will and not having any conditions on our service for Him. I thought about this and realised that I had my ears open waiting to hear where Rae McLellan (whom I had met at MTC) was going to go. So, I told God I would go wherever, no matter what happened with Rae. Almost instantly, it was if I heard a voice saying, "Kalimantan". (Kalimantan is the Indonesian part of the island of Borneo.)

Near the end of the two year college course, I was considering what the next step was. I felt that I should go into WEC Candidates' Course after the Christmas holidays. Candidates' Course was a six month course required of all applicants who wanted to enter the WEC as missionaries. Up until then, WEC didn't accept male candidates straight from Bible Colleges. They required them to do a year's pastoral service in a church before going to Candidates' Course. When I approached Mr Dinnen I was in trepidation but much relieved to hear that WEC had just changed their policy and now men could do Candidates Course first and then do the year pastoral work once accepted. God had not misled me!

It was during my time in Sydney WEC HQ doing the last three months of candidates' course that my money, earnt on a farm at Copping, Tasmania at the finish of MTC, finally ran out. We were expected to put some money each week into the common purse if we were able. It was a literal purse kept in a drawer in a store room. It was done like that so no one knew who put money in and who did not.

One Sunday after lunch I got a phone call from Reg Baggs (a staff member) who had a part-time pastorate in a Baptist church kilometres away. He wanted me to come down for the evening service and to give a testimony and I said, "Yes". I didn't tell him that I had no money. So I spent some time in prayer that afternoon but still no money. It came time to leave so I walked down to the bus stop and the bus came and went and still no money. I walked back to HQ but couldn't let Reg know I wasn't coming as he would not have been near a phone. Next day he saw me and I explained my position and he said that he had guessed what had happened. He gave me a small gift. One of the other candidates heard of it and came and told me that she felt she should have given me money that previous afternoon but hadn't. However she went away still without giving me money. This was one of my first lessons in faith in regards to finance.

Small gifts came in and I was able to contribute something to the common purse. I can't remember if I was able to give the full amount or not each week. But this was the start of trusting the Lord to meet my needs without asking anyone but Him to help. (This was the official policy of WEC for all its work and for all its workers.) Rae and I were writing to each other by this time and discussing the future. Towards the end of my time at Candidates' Course in Sydney I was praying about the fare home to Brisbane, Queensland, as well as buying an engagement ring. Rae had said that a ring was not necessary as we would still be engaged without a ring. However I still felt that the Lord would supply the wherewithal for us to have one. I think it was only a couple of weeks or so before the end of the course that a fairly large cheque arrived in the mail from some friends in Tasmania. When I was in Tasmania they had set aside a calf for me and, seeing it was now saleable, they sold it and sent me the money. None of this I knew of course. They did not know my situation and I had not heard from them for a while so it was good timing on God's part. It was enough to get me home to Brisbane and to buy an engagement ring. We were married in December 1973.

In preparation for heading off to Kalimantan I arranged a trip to the southern parts of Australia, mostly to visit my friends from air force days. WEC had arranged some meetings but it was mostly personal visits that I did. I didn't have much money in hand when I left nor did Rae. She stayed home in Gympie, where we were living at the time, with the twins (Caleb and Murray born in 1975) who were about one year old. The first stop was Beaudesert Baptist Church where I stayed with the Hohls. They owned their own plumbing business. As I was leaving for Newcastle the next morning he told me to fill my car up from his petrol bowser. The church gave me a cash gift as well. If it had been a cheque I would not have had enough resources to get to Newcastle.

I spent a few days in Newcastle catching up with various friends and telling them what we were going to do. Some gave me gifts so I had enough to get me to Sydney-the next stop-but not to Wagga Wagga which was the stop after that. In Sydney I visited a couple of friends. The gifts I was given were enough to get me to Wagga Wagga but not to Melbourne. I stayed with some old friends in Wagga Wagga and caught up with various friends. Once again I was given enough to get to Melbourne where I stayed in the WEC HQ. I spent probably about a week in Melbourne before heading back home. Once again I was given enough for this trip and even had some over once I arrived in Gympie. The Lord had provided for Rae and the boys in my absence as well. I might add that none of these gifts were solicited. None of the people who gave knew our needs either.

We spent ten wonderful, and sometimes hard years, in Kalimantan. We arrived in Pontianak, the regional capital of West Kalimantan, in May 1976. We had a year of language study ahead of us there.

We waited and waited for our luggage (eighteen pieces) to turn up but it was well past the expected time of about a month after our arrival and no news. We wrote to Singapore, Surabaya in Java and Brisbane but got no definite news back. The ship was supposed to have been delayed etc. We did hear that the Missionary Children's School at Serukam, north of Pontianak, run by the Conservative Baptists, had lost 12 drums of books and school materials but thought nothing of it. Finally in September we wrote home and asked Rae's Dad to look into it. After investigating he sent a telegram to the Intermission Business Office in Jakarta who radioed Missionary Aviation Fellowship (MAF) in Pontianak. An American MAF couple came around to give us the bad news. We later found out the details. The Indonesian ship, Dirgantana II, carrying our goods from Singapore to Pontianak had collided with an oil tanker in fog just outside of Singapore harbour and so our goods were at the bottom of the South China Sea.

Rae wrote home on 19th September just after we received the news, "We still haven't had the courage to go through our itemised list but it has been bad enough just recalling some of the goods. Besides smaller items, we had a fridge; sewing machine; two tape recorders; cassette/radio you gave us for our wedding; duplicator (Roneo); two outboard motors (one 25 hp and the other a 1 ¼ hp Gulpy); five new rubber mattresses; five nets (mosquito) made up in a special style; about $600.00 of lovely new tools; sheets; pillowcases; quilt; towels; kitchenware – dinner sets, cutlery sets, tea sets, saucepans, ovenware, a lovely supply of Tupperware – so handy in this humidity; a great stack of medical goods from the chemist; four blankets …..; my precious Buchanan tartan rug; …."

It certainly was a loss yet we felt too that the Lord had somehow prepared us for it. While we were shocked at the news it did not throw us. We wondered why the Lord would take it all when He had provided it so wonderfully. However He did so again.

Missionaries from all the missions in Kalbar started to give us things. They even put on a shower evening for us as well. When people back home heard about it money flowed in. We found that we didn't need to buy much in Australia as it was almost all available in Pontianak at a cheaper price. Of course we could not replace our wedding presents. Eventually we did get three drums of goods sent from Australia that we could not buy there but by that time we had moved inland. They were sent by my Dad from Brisbane in January and we should have got them well before we moved into the interior. They actually did arrive a couple of weeks before we moved but it took about four weeks to clear them through customs and eventually MAF flew them to us a couple of weeks after we arrived in Nanga Lebang (the mission HQ in the interior). So the Lord wonderfully provided for us again.

We had our first furlough five years after our arrival in Kalimantan. (We had had a two month holiday in the middle of this term to meet up with Rae's sister and family who were missionaries with WEC in Venezuela, then home on furlough.)

On arrival home we found out that Rae's Dad had bought an old EH Holden for us to use while on furlough. It served us very well. Also we knew that he was looking for a place for us to stay. He found a house for us to rent in Phoenix Street, Gympie. It was immediately behind the One Mile State School where Rae had done her early years of schooling. It cost us $60 a week in rent – an impossible figure for us. Many times in Kalimantan we didn't get too much more than that in one month but always sufficient. However the Lord was very faithful as we were only ever late once for a payment in the ten months we were in the house. We normally paid the rent on a Saturday and that time we did it on the Monday as we had to get a cheque cleared. Most weeks we had the money at the beginning of the week, quite a few times it was

Friday when it arrived and a few times it was Saturday. Of course no one knew our situation. God simply answered prayer.

After serving two terms in Kalimantan we felt it was time for us to return home. After a few months break WEC asked us to serve on the MTC staff with responsibility for the catering. We served there for five years.

Particularly towards the end of each year we would be praying for guidance for the next year. Our original agreement was for a year but year after year we felt no leading to leave. Finally after nearly five years at MTC we felt that the Lord had given us a green light. I wrote away to a few family and friends in Queensland enquiring as to any opportunities in pastorates there. We wanted to be a bit closer to our parents – especially to my Dad who was getting quite sick. A day or so before my letter to Noel Wilcox arrived, he had handed in his resignation as Pastor at Tent Hill Baptist. Noel was from Rae's home church in Gympie. I had visited the Tent Hill church on deputation but did not know if Noel and Bev were still there or not. The timely arrival of my letter struck a chord with the leadership of the church.

We had eleven busy years in the pastorate in Tent Hill. It was a blessing to see how the Lord met the needs of the church at Tent Hill. We opened the newly built manse with a smallish debt and I think it only took the church about two years to clear it. At times the finances got really low but we never saw the church in debt. Once the church got down to $250 in the bank but the Lord kept us. We had other times too when the bank was low. We put on Matt French as my associate pastor part time for a while but then not long after that full time. There was no way we could have met his wage but the giving increased and we had no trouble. We had similar stories when we put on his replacement Arthur Bray and then after him Stewart Pieper. The church always gave over ten percent to missions and other Christian work even when funds were low.

In late October 2002 I gave the Tent Hill church three months' notice. That meant that when we finished our ministry on Sunday 26th January 2003 we were short of eleven years of service there by about two weeks. We had been praying about what to do for a few years and would have resigned beforehand but never felt that it was the Lord's time to do so. Now that time had arrived. It was confirmed to us by two phone calls. The day after I announced my resignation to the Elders I received a phone call from a church asking if I would consider their pastorate and the next day another from another church. One of them was Longreach Baptist where I was to eventually do a short interim ministry. Neither of these churches knew of my resignation.

There are many more instances of the Lord's provision and guidance over the years that I could tell of. Truly God has been gracious to us. Praise Him!

6. AM I NOT ABLE TO TAKE CARE OF YOU?

I know of four women in our fellowship that have had to face the diagnosis of breast cancer. Each woman has had a very different oath to walk. Dell Windolf bears tells of her journey of faith as she dealt with the diagnosis and treatment.

Boxing Day 2015, 5.30 am, I discovered something different about my right breast. My beloved insisted I needed to get it checked out. I'd had a breast screen mammogram on August 11th 2015, only four and a half months prior and it was reported to me as "No sign of Breast cancer detected."

Due to holidays, we had to wait until the following Tuesday to see our GP. (You note I say, "we" for that's what it has been, my husband and I together). One of the Lord's many blessings to me is a supportive husband but also he had an infected cyst on his neck so we were having double appointments. This rarely happened in our 48 years of marriage.

Tuesday 29th December 2015, I saw my GP and he sent me for a breast scan and a biopsy in Gatton. He was hoping they would do it that day. However, they couldn't do those procedures until the following week. I went back to the surgery and was booked into another radiology clinic in Ipswich for the next morning, Wednesday 30th December.

The next decision was when to tell the family, before or after tests. We asked the Lord to guide us to make the right choice. Late Tuesday evening it all fell into place and the family were told. I've no doubt that my boys and girls began to pray for I believe I saw what the Lord did for me the next day.

At the radiology clinic in Ipswich I waited my turn. When it came, I handed over my referral only to be told very firmly by the receptionist I had not booked in properly. I would receive only the breast scan because that's all I had booked in for. The biopsy could not be done that day as they were fully booked and I would need to make another appointment. She spoke to me almost as if I was of little understanding. I sat down rather meekly and waited and was called in soon after that. I hope that that receptionist survived the day because, after walking through the door into the radiology rooms, I received a great deal of care and attention.

First....Breast scan. The radiologist called a colleague to come see me at the end of the scan and it happened to be the doctor who would read the pictures. He asked questions. I answered them, then he made the statement, "Your doctor will probably want you to have a mammogram." He left. I was instructed to wait in my little cubby hole.

Second..... Eventually my girl came by and said, "You will be a little while but we are organising a mammogram for you." I found out later they rang my GP for his consent.

The radiologist this time was following specific guidelines for the pictures. She left while I waited then came back and said, "He wants one more." This was done differently. She left again and returned with the words, "That's all he wants. You can take a seat and wait but don't get dressed."

Third..... More waiting, my girl came by to say," We are shuffling things around and we will be doing the biopsy soon." I was called in and I was asked to sign a form which I did. The doctor entered again directing the procedure choosing one of the fatty tissue sites. He asked me if I'd signed the form. I said, "Yes." It was for them to access my breast screen pictures from Queensland Health.

I walked out of those rooms one and three quarter hours later. Hopefully their care and determination to find answers didn't disrupt too many other people. As I have said, I hope the receptionist survived.

We entered our GP's office for the results later that day. He shrugged his shoulders and said the scan and the mammogram did not show cancer. Being New Year long weekend we were instructed to make an appointment for Monday to get the results of the biopsy. We left the surgery with the doctor all smiles telling us to have a good weekend. Unknown to us, our doctor received the results late Thursday before he left the surgery. He told us he'd thought about ringing us but as there was nothing to be done before Monday and we had an appointment for Monday he decided to wait to give us the news together and face to face. We both appreciated his thoughtfulness.

Monday 4th January 2016, the day we learned I have breast cancer. Our GP was very caring explaining the best way forward both medically as well as emotionally. Being January, most surgeons are on holidays but the one he had chosen for me was back at work the following week. I could have gone to Brisbane but our GP felt that, for us, we would "be more comfortable with Toowoomba" and he certainly was right. He also told me I was a lucky woman that they found the cancer as it could easily have been missed and I should count my blessings. It wasn't hard to identify some of those blessings.

Monday 11th January 2016 we met my surgeon. He is kind, gentle, respectful, truthful and explained the options as well as the risks so we were able to make informed decisions. Having been under his care in hospital I've learned he is very protective towards his patients. I was scheduled for surgery on 21st January for a mastectomy.

Thursday 21st January 2016, 7 o'clock at the day surgery at St Andrew's Hospital for admittance and scan plus injection of some radioactive "stuff" to find the leader lymph nodes. Fascinating technology, we surely are, 'fearfully and wonderfully made'.

All those procedures were completed by 9.30 am and my surgery was scheduled for 1.30 pm. I found myself waiting in the day surgery area but not for long. I was soon asked if I would like to go to my room to which I said, "Yes please".

Surgery went well. However, the leader lymph nodes tested positive to cancer so my surgeon advised a second operation to remove more nodes. Six days after the first operation I was back in surgery for a shorter but much, much sorer surgery. The lymph nodes removed in that op tested negative to cancer. The second operation certainly has taken its toll on me but I am mending. I have an appointment to see my oncology doctor on Thursday 11th February 2016.

So where has the Lord been through all of this? He has been in it all directing those who have the skills and training to help me. He has surrounded me with people to love me, to pray for me and He has been there day by day reminding me of his love and care for me as I've read my daily reading from *Jesus Calling* by Sarah Young.

I share just one of these readings from January 18th, "I am leading you along the high road, but there are descents as well as ascents. In the distance you see snow-covered peeks glistening in brilliant sunlight. Your longing to reach those peaks is good, but you must not take shortcuts. Your assignment is to follow Me, allowing Me to direct your path. Let the heights beckon you onward, but stay close to me.

Learn to trust Me when things go " wrong". Disruptions to your routine highlight your dependence on Me. Trusting acceptance of trials brings blessings that far outweigh them all. Walk hand and hand with Me through this day. I have lovingly planned every step of the way. Trust does not falter when the path becomes rocky and steep. Breathe deep draughts of My Presence, and hold tightly to My hand. Together we can make it." I remind myself constantly, hold tightly to his hand, for together with him we can make it!

Many family friends and strangers were praying for me from all over Queensland and overseas. God is good all the time, even on the days one wonders what he's doing. You see, my beloved sister was bed ridden as the result of the stroke she'd had in July 2015 but she had remained very, very clear minded but was now not expected to live. She was given two to three days, just before the four doses of what my oncologist warned me would be 'the rough chemotherapy'. The timing seemed less than perfect but who are we to question the Maker of the Universe who knows the end from the beginning.

He had already given me the answer to the question, should my treatment be postponed until things had settled down, you see before this all happened I believe the Lord gave me the answer when I remembered the words I'd read, "Continue on this path with Me, enjoying My presence even in adversity I am always before you, as well as alongside you, See Me beckoning to you: "Come!

follow Me." So we changed nothing and sadly my sister entered Paradise 24 hours before my first chemo treatment. My sister and I spoke with each other on the telephone the day before she died, then again on morning of her death. Though she never responded, I was able to tell her again how much I loved and admired her and goodbye one more time and I'd meet her on the streets of gold, and about 10 minutes later she left her earthly body.

Chemotherapy day arrived and the drugs dripped into a vein via a smart port inserted under the skin by my right shoulder. We came home waiting to see how chemo would affect me. My beloved husband made sure I followed all the instructions I was given. Tuesday morning I struggled to have breakfast so I could have my prescribed medications for I was feeling terrible. I stumbled back to the bedroom and as I was struggling to get onto the bed I sensed a round shaped presence roll into the room and stop beside me. I sensed rather than heard what it said, " You'd be better off dead." I admit to agreeing with that idea because I felt dreadful. The round type presence left and has never ever returned. Praise God.

Did I feel better? No, I got worse and was advised to go to oncology where several medical personnel tried to work out what was wrong with me. They asked me for my name. I think I knew it but it was just out of my reach. As for my date of birth, no idea if I managed to tell them. I was admitted to hospital on a sodium drip as my sodium level had dropped so low I was close to a seizure but the Lord didn't allow that to happen. I believe normal sodium level should be between 135-145; mine was 113. My blood pressure dropped and I was not allowed out of bed so I was taken off my BP medication. I was home in three days but could not attend my sister's funeral.

I'd been asking if I could be put into hospital after the next chemo just in case but was getting "No" for an answer and assured it was unlikely to happen again. However, I sincerely believe the Lord had other plans and answered prayer. I saw my surgeon before my second treatment. His regular treatment nurse was sick and, who was in her place, none other than my breast care nurse who knew all the details of my recent stay in hospital. She also informed him I was anxious that it could happen again and wanted to be in hospital for observation after the next treatment. It took him just one phone call and a few words to secure a bed for me. Remember what the Lord told me, "Hold tightly to my hand and together we will make it". Thank you Lord.

Second treatment day arrived. My chemo nurse took my BP then left me with the words, "I'll need to talk to the doctor." I then looked up and saw my BP on the machine which was right in front of me and, having been treated for high BP for years, I was aware of what was an acceptable level and those numbers were far from acceptable. Chemo went ahead, sodium drip went ahead, plus BP medication was reintroduced along with lectures on not stressing over my BP as it was really not my problem but a problem for my doctors to solve. Yeah! Right. Three days later I arrived home and never did make the last step onto the veranda but tripped and fell full body length, face down across the veranda. So off to the doctor to get checked out. Apart from bruises and broken glasses I was whole, no broken skin so no risk of infection, a deviated septum but no broken bones. We were praising the Lord for His protection. Also praised Him that my glasses were replaced without a test as the chemo was affecting my eyesight. However, I had trouble with my thinking. At times, it seemed I couldn't control it and think straight. May God bless my husband who often held my hand and prayed. I blamed chemo but couldn't really find anyone to agree with me on that thought but it was driving me crazy. My oncologist suggested a psychologist and antidepressant. I saw a Christian psychologist and he was very encouraging. Friends were asking how to pray and my request was for relief from my screwed up head.

Chemo three and back in hospital with sodium drip, home again still dealing with my mind as well as the effects of chemo. I remember the day I cried out aloud to the Lord to take away the torment in my mind. Days went by and on Monday, seven days before my fourth chemo when I should have been feeling better, I was getting worse so saw my GP. I was the one to suggest the antidepressant even though my breast care nurse didn't believe I was depressed. But I was desperate. Home again, but rather than improve I got even worse. I felt so weak and frail I fully expected the fourth chemo to kill me if I was treated. Midday Thursday I was back to the doctor with all my confusing symptoms only to be told it was probably the antidepressant as it would take about two weeks for my body to adjust and for it to have the required effect.

Home to bed. A couple hours later I became aware that my beloved was talking to someone on the telephone. He soon came into me and told me he'd rung the doctor and in very short time I was on my way to hospital in Gatton to see if they could work out what was causing my trouble. Going to Gatton hospital was a massive answer to prayer ,not only to my prayers but to the prayers of many others. My sodium level was 114 this time. The doctor dealt with my immediate need for sodium. He must have spent the night researching the records of my blood tests and medications so before I left the hospital the antidepressant was removed because it leeched out sodium.

A change was made in other medication for the same reason plus I was prescribed six salt tablets a day and I was restricted to one and a half litres of fluid a day. The doctor's words to me were, "I wouldn't normally leave any of my patients out of hospital with a sodium level of 121 but you're so used to operating at low levels you'll handle it," and I did. Praise God the six salt tablets a day and restricted fluid did their jobs really well because on the Monday my sodium was 130 and my head was clear. I felt normal again and apparently family and friends noticed and, I might add, the antidepressant was never reintroduced. Yes, chemo was still rough and caused effects, but my head and thinking was so much better. I didn't feel like I was going crazy. Praise the Lord.

Three weeks later I started the weekly chemo which in my naivety I thought would be easier, but discovered the guarded comments of my breast care nurse proved she left a lot unsaid. I was to have twelve treatments although my oncologist said she might reduce it to ten. The only day of the week that came close to being a good day was Monday treatment day. I was longing to hear my treatment being reduced to ten as I struggled with the effects of chemo.

This is what I read a few days before my sixth treatment, "Keep walking with Me along the path I have chosen for you. Your desire to live close to Me is a delight to My heart. I could instantly grant you your spiritual riches you desire, but that is not My way for you. Together we will forge a pathway up the high mountain. The journey is arduous at times, and you are weak. Someday you will dance light-footed on high peaks; but for now your walk is often plodding and heavy. All I require of you is to take the next step, clinging to My hand for strength and direction. Though the path is difficult and the scenery dull at the moment, there are sparkling surprises just around the bend. Stay on the path I have selected for you. It truly is the path of Life."

On the sixth treatment day I was told my treatment had been reduced to ten. It seemed like a sparkling surprise to me. By the time I'd had my eighth treatment the tingling and numbing in my hands and feet were getting worse. I remember asking the Lord to give my oncologist wisdom to be able to make wise decisions regarding my treatment and when we arrived for treatment nine we were told my chemo was complete. They would not push my body any more. My beloved and I sat there like stunned mullets. Although it was a relief, suddenly it was as if we'd lost direction and I discovered it wasn't the euphoric event I expected. One does not recover from chemo as quickly as one would like. I had three months before I started the 25 treatments of radiation which, compared to chemo, was almost a non event. However, it had its challenges.

Only the Lord knows all the details of this journey and without him it would have been unbearable. I value my family, friends and strangers who prayed. May the Lord bless each one. A habit I got into was going to bed around six pm with my iPad and I listened to lots of good preachers and gospel music via YouTube. The other habit my beloved and I got into early in this cancer journey was, when he came to bed, he'd read the Bible or Study notes to me. Then we'd hold hands and pray. We still have our quiet time together like this and though last year our prayers were a little self-centred our prayers now include many things but always others who are on a journey with cancer.

The joy and thanks to the Lord, the day I could go onto the veranda and the floorboards didn't seem to curve or rise up and buckle; the day I realised I could read the answers to the questions on The Chase TV program; the day my eyes stop strobing if I looked at the wooden blinds the wrong way; when my feet an ankles stopped feeling like the size of footballs in bed at night. Although even eleven months since chemo they still feel numb. The joy to be able to hold fabric properly again while I sew. And actually just feeling well. We take so many things for granted. There were many other joyous milestones.

Another thing I clearly remember was my GP telling me the first day he told us of the cancer, "You will be poked and prodded for the rest of your life."

I treasure the day the Lord reminded me, 'I created the world and flung the stars into space, I made you and know everything about you, am I not able to take care of you?'

I also asked Del's beloved, Sel, for a testimony. It is the shortest but extremely profound. "If you do not stray you don't have to return."

7 TRANSITION TO RETIREMENT

Steve and Robyn, Christchurch NZ in the background Feb 2017

Steven and Robyn Beasley have been very close friends of the editor for many years. We have shared many of life's dramas and grown old together.

After eight years of fortnightly working trips to Papua New Guinea four times a year, and spending most weekends away from Gatton, our lives changed direction. With none of our children living in Australia at that time and my working life coming towards the finishing line, we knew we needed to wait on the Lord regarding our future and the journey into older age and retirement.

A pleasant visit with Reg and Heather Crust sowed a seed in us individually and, on the way home, we both said we felt led to make Tenthill Baptist Church our Church in the meantime. We were kindly received by the Church family and found the Sunday morning drive to Tenthill an uplifting and blessed journey. The drive out in the country was a time of blessing as we saw the beauty of God's creation and the changing crops being grown, especially when the country had rain. The beautiful surroundings are a joy to behold and the Church in the Potato (or Lettuce) Patch brought us closer to the Creator.

We were blessed by the music and singing every Sunday and we found Pastor Iain Russell's messages both challenging and encouraging; they ministered to us in a powerful way. The Church ministry was very practical and relevant to life and aimed to reach out to the local community and be caring and involved in the community. The fellowship at the morning tea after the service every week was as good as the morning tea itself and that couldn't be any better!

We were blessed in the knowledge that Pastor Iain waited on God and followed His leading. Why else would an avid fisherman leave the coast at Agnes Waters and come to Tenthill unless God's call was much more important than catching fish? It's more important to be a fisher of men than to be a fisherman.

We were blessed by the Church family as we became part of their lives. Opportunities for serving arose with Kids' Holiday Club and Kids' Hope.

I finished up work and was able to be more involved in helping with the computer and PA system and then as Church Treasurer where it was a blessing to see younger members of the Church Family being involved.

We had known that we would move from Gatton when I retired and we had made a decision when we had none of our children in Australia that we would downsize into a smaller unit in a Retirement Village. Finally, the time was right for the move and we left the Tenthill Baptist Church and moved to Toowoomba where we have a new Frontline.

8 THE CROOKED MADE STRAIGHT

Grayton and Shan Tranter, when not enjoying the good light in Broome, Western Australia living in their caravan on the beach, spend part of the year with their daughter, son-in-law and grandchildren on a vegetable farm at Tenthill. During these times they enjoyed fellowship at the church in the potato field . In his own words, Grayton tells of a miracle that transformed his life.

I was brought up on a potato farm in the 1950's at Trentham, Victoria digging potatoes with a fork into 150 lb[6] bags which, for a sixteen year old, was very heavy. I could pick one up by myself but mostly with my brother, one each side and lift it on to a truck or trailer. After a few years, I started to get a crook back which began a history of going to chiropractors. In the mid 1960's I left the farm for a while. Sometimes I couldn't push down the pedals on a truck. I moved to South Australia in 1975 with my brother to a potato farm at Coonawarra.

In the early 1980's I was visiting a chiropractor once a week. If I heard of a chiropractor who relieved someone else's pain I would go whether it was in Hamilton, Horsham or Mt Gambier[7]. I visited a chiropractor in Mt Gambier every week for two years. I then went to a chiropractor in Naracoorte. I was waiting one week and the receptionist gave me the notes to take in. I counted up the visits, 101 times I had visited that chiropractor. It always seemed to be temporary relief. Many times in this period I would climb into the backseat of the car for my wife to take me to the chiropractor only to be told that they could not do anything for me because my back would be too inflamed.

I got to the stage that I said to my wife Shanragh, "I can't keep

---

6 About 68 kg. These bags were a common site in the valley in my youth and ruined the backs of many farmers and truckies.

7 The distance from Mt Gambia to Horsham is 216k.

going farming." Getting out of bed of a morning was rolling off the bed onto the floor and pulling myself up the dresser. At this time I was going to church in Penola, South Australia.[8] At church, we had a very charismatic priest (Father Don Coots) who had been praying for people. For a few Sundays he had been saying we would have a Sunday praying for people who would come forward. Driving to church, it was agony getting out of the car and brought tears to my eyes. Walking through the back door to the back seat, I was feeling about as low as I could get. Father Don called people to come forward but I didn't have the guts to get up in front of everyone, nor did I feel like it.

He persisted in encouraging people to come forward. Some did. Anyway, everyone prayed. Getting towards the end of the service he said he had an awareness of someone being healed. I didn't feel any different then. At the end of the service he said stand up and say last prayers. I stood up without thinking, then I realized I had no pain! I bent over to the right, left. I realized the pain was gone and I felt like I was on fire, heat came up from my lower back and stomach up through my head and out. I realized I was healed. I got outside the door. A friend I knew was standing there. I said, "I reckon my back was healed."

"That's good. Who won the footy yesterday?" I knew he wasn't very interested so I told some others who were there who were a bit more attentive to my excitement. I have never had a crook back from that day.

Twelve months later I twisted my neck so I went to Naracoorte to the chiropractor. I went in and he said, "Where have you been?"

I said, "Do you believe in miracles?"

He said, "Some."

---

8 50k north of Mt Gambier.

I said, "I was healed in church 12 months ago."

Skeptically he said, "On the couch, we'll see." Going from my feet to my neck, his exact words were, "It's certainly different there."

I said. "I told you I was healed."

So thank you God through his son, our saviour, Yeshua, the messiah, for all his love and healing. Praise YHWH. Sometimes, I have tears thinking of his miracles of healing, my back and other miracles he has done for me.

Footnote: During the prayer service when Father Don Coots called for people to go forward, one family got up and walked out. They never came back. The reason given was that a mere man couldn't pray for people to be healed. Only God could do that. This showed me that the Devil puts terrible things in peoples' mind.

9 THE HEALING POWER OF FORGIVENESS

A testimony of God's goodness during April 2015 to December 2017

My name is Julian. I am married to Del, blessed with four children and a pet budgie. Below is a testimony of my life experience from April, 2015 to December, 2017. In 2014, I graduated from the University of Southern Queensland with a Bachelor of Education. I trained as a primary teacher.

At the end of March, 2015 I was contacted by the Deputy Principal of Charters Towers School of Distance Education. He offered me a full-time, permanent position teaching Year Seven classes. I accepted. I did not research or investigate this position. I assumed I would see students through a computer screen and lessons would involve lots of learning conversations and fun. I immediately began packing and preparing for the move from the Lockyer Valley to North Queensland.

I commenced the teaching position on the 20th April but was not aware I would be teaching Year Eight Science and Year Nine IT Core until my position started. This came as a shock. My Head of Department assured me that the Year Eight students and Year Nine students had learning difficulties and abilities of primary age students. I believed her. I embarked on preparing lessons for these students.

However, once I began teaching, teaching and learning in the setting of Distance Education took a fair amount of time to comprehend. The setting of Distance Education is very different to mainstream classroom teaching which I have been trained for. For example, the teacher and students enter into the classroom by logging into a program called Blackboard Collaborate where the teacher and students view a screen with touch tools on the left hand side and the remainder of the screen filled with teacher constructed PowerPoint slides. The teacher and students cannot see each other but only hear each other during a classroom lesson. This set-up frustrated me because I could not see the students, their interactions with me and their student cohort. It was very hard to understand whether they were actually learning or not during class time. You could not see them. I am motivated by people's physical reactions to me.

As I settled into the teaching position I received constant criticism and very little encouragement after teaching a batch of lessons. I started developing health problems. I visited the doctor and received medication for anxiety (which also caused insomnia). This affected my teaching practice. The mentor I was assigned did not treat me with respect nor did she provide many opportunities of guidance and modelling. This did not allow me to grow as a teacher but led to further stress, tension and questioning of my abilities. From the outset I did not receive guiding and modelling, just feedback and some discussion after a batch of lessons had been taught. At Charters Towers, on two occasions a senior teacher observed me in a lesson. The first lesson involved no student's attendance so the lesson was recorded and, for the second lesson, there were three students which was exam preparation with very little teaching. There was no change in the school's support mechanisms despite being placed at risk six months into teaching with constant critical feedback and no guiding or modelling. I responded by implementing their feedback in my teaching approach immediately and asked fellow teachers but the school's response continued to be the same: constant critical feedback, no guiding or modelling. Very frustrating!

I endeavoured to be prepared for lessons and provided continued effort in all of my planning and teaching. I worked half of my weekends and five hours each night preparing PowerPoints and breathing life into the lessons. I got up in the mornings regularly by 5 am. These hours intruded on my family time and my own health.

At the beginning of December 2015, my employment at Charters Towers School of Distance Education was terminated. On the same day my employment was terminated, my wife received her old teaching job back at Peace Lutheran School, Gatton. We applied for financial and logistical support from the Queensland Education Department for support moving ourselves and our belongings back to the Lockyer Valley. It was refused. Praise the Lord, family provided monetary support to help pay for costs to move back. It's expensive to move!

At the beginning of February or March 2016, I received notification from the Queensland College of Teachers of an investigation into my time at Charters Towers. The QCT was ascertaining whether there were grounds for disciplinary action. I was to submit evidence as part of the investigation. This was in response to allegations of incompetence as a teacher after my employment was terminated at the Charters Towers School of Distance Education by the Queensland Department of Education and Training (DET) in December 2015. Firstly in February 2016, the QCT requested a requirement for information to satisfy grounds for disciplinary action. I and the DET supplied information to the QCT. This information was evaluated by the QCT against the Australian Professional Standards for Teachers (APST) at the graduate level. Secondly in July 2016, the QCT advised me of a notice of disciplinary investigation and allegations about my performance against the APST standards. I was to respond with a written submission highlighting my knowledge of the standards with examples from my teaching experience. Thirdly, in October 2016, I received notification that the investigation was complete and the written report was handed to the Professional Practice and Conduct Committee (PPC Committee). Fourthly, in February 2017, the PPC Committee determined I failed to meet six APST standards for graduate level. I was given the choice of an oral hearing or a written submission to the Committee regarding the matter. I elected to provide a written submission highlighting my knowledge of the standards with examples from my teaching practice. Lastly in June 2017, I received written correspondence from the PPC Committee which determined that grounds for disciplinary action against me did not exist. The case was closed. Praise the Lord!

The Good Lord has been my help and my shield during this time. I memorised Psalm 23 which helped calm my nerves at night to help me to sleep during the course of the investigation.

Since returning from Charters Towers at the end of 2015, our Youth Pastor and his wife immediately asked me and the family over for a meal. During the course of the meal, we discussed my experience at Charters Towers. He shared that he and his family experienced a similar experience at one of the Churches he worked at in the past. As I learned I was under investigation during 2016, he recommended that I advocate for a written copy of the outcome of the investigation.

Religious Instruction rehabilitated me as a teacher. One of my goals when moving back to the Lockyer Valley at the end of 2015 was to teach Religious Instruction for 2016. My Pastor was fully aware of my experience at Charters Towers. For 2016, he took me under his wing and mentored me. For a whole term, he guided and modelled teaching lessons for Religious Instruction. Coupled with my teaching training this empowered me. I took over the teaching of his classes and, for the rest of the school year, I taught Religious Instruction. This experience has given me the confidence to continue moving forward as a teacher.

I have learned much about Rugby League players when they have handled failure. Wade Graham completed a high tackle against Johnathan Thurston and was found guilty by the Rugby League Judiciary. This ruled him out of State of Origin contention. Wade Graham was devastated. The New South Wales Coach Laurie Daley encouraged him to be confident in his abilities and to keep moving forward as a player. Wade Graham has followed this advice and last I heard he scored four tries in an international test match, equaling the record!

I have learnt from The Voice artists who have handled failure. An opera singer discussed with Boy George about his lack of support from the audience when singing with the operatic group The 10 Tenors. This experience knocked the artist's confidence in his abilities. He subsequently quit touring with the group. The opera singer believed he deserved another chance at singing and auditioned for the show. Boy George commented that The Voice judges and audience were right behind him.

An elder of the Church invited me out for a cuppa and cake. He shared with me his experience of anxiety and trauma after his dismissal in the leadership team in another Church family through no fault of his own. He also advised me whatever the outcome of the investigation to have it written down.

I have learnt the power of forgiveness. For much of the month of November 2017, I have been busy preparing documentation to update my teacher registration. This has involved outlining the scene at Charters Towers and subsequent investigation. This brought back enormous feelings of anxiety and trauma. Our Church received a guest speaker who preached about the Unmerciful Servant in Matthew 18:21-35. As I finalised the documentation for the registration, a family member asked whether I had forgiven the scene at Charters and blessed those involved. I realised I had not. I forgave and blessed those individuals. Since forgiving and blessing those involved with my bad experience, I have felt a terrific sense of relief and joy which has replaced feelings of anxiety and trauma. Another family member instructed me that I will need to forgive whenever I approach similar situations.

I am very much thankful for family and friends helping me and the family during this season of life. At Church, people would ask about the scene and say that were praying for me and encouraging me with words of hope for the future. I am thankful for the elder in our Church who encouraged me to write a testimony of this experience which you are reading.

I am still determined to teach and grow in belief in my abilities. I am still unaware why the good Lord brought me through this experience but with further life experience I believe all will be revealed.

10 THE UPS AND DOWNS OF A BOY FROM THE DOWNS

The Rev. Dr Alan Gordon, along with his wife Rosemary served Tenthill Baptist Church from2005? to 2006. Unfortunately, our church had suffered a split and Alan had been trained to bring healing to churches that had undergone difficult times. It was termed an Intentional Interim Ministry and is intended to be short and prepare the church for a brighter future under a new pastor.

Alan encouraged me to take up my books again and study for my Master of Biblical Studies.

I was walking with two men by my side and a hearse following. One man asked, "You are from Millmerran, our home town. We can't remember you. Who is your dad?"

"Don Gordon."

"He's a good man. He owned a garage. But we still can't remember you. Who were your friends?"

I mentioned their names and the startled response was, "That was the worst gang that Millmerran ever had. How can you be part of that gang and yet become a minister?"

I replied, "I was the worst person in that gang." They just shook their heads in amazement.

Years later, I made the mistake of taking my wife Rosemary to a Millmerran School reunion. Rosemary mixed with my old friends. As we drove away, she was very quiet. Eventually, she said, "You told me that you were bad when you were young, but I never dreamed that you were that bad."

What changed me was that I became a Christian. But that occurred in stages.

I went to a Presbyterian Camp. On an excursion, I saw a cliff and noticed that it had a large series little ledges jutting out that were perfect for climbing. I suggested to those around, "Let's climb up to the top." When we came to an end of the little ledges, I dug into the firm, wet sand, and the sturdy hand-holds then became sturdy foot-holds. But, almost at the top, the sand was very dry and would never be able to hold our weight. So we had to return.

As I was first up, I was last down. The other climbers had loosened the hand and foot-holds. All four gave way on me at the same time. I looked down to the huge bounders below. I prayed, "God, if you save me, you can have my life." As soon as the prayer finished, I was falling past the only root in that section of the cliff. My right hand reached out and I could only grasp the thin root by two fingers.

I sought to fulfil my part of the bargain, God could have my life. Have you ever tried to live a Christian life without being born again? I tried, but on return to Millmerran the old gang's practices began to drag me down again.

At that stage, my Dad's garage in Millmerran burned down, and he purchased a farm at Rywung, west of Chinchilla. On my first day on the farm, my Dad and I were walking through the tall grass. Suddenly, I couldn't put my left foot down on the ground. So I stood back and looked. My next step would have taken me onto a coiled death adder. It was obvious that God's hand was on me, before I was a Christian.

Before the end of that year, in a car coming home from a Sunday night church service, I asked my mother what the preacher meant with words like, 'born again, salvation, regeneration, and just believe.' My mother's response was that of a teacher: "Jesus died for you. He wants you to invite Him into your life." It happened in that car on that night.

As Chinchilla had no high school, Dad sent me to Toowoomba Grammar School. One Sunday afternoon most of the school was elsewhere playing cricket against other schools. I was leaning on the massive water tank next to the top sporting oval reading a Christian book. Suddenly, I heard a clear voice, "Alan, run!" In a flash, I was on my feet at full pace with my book in front of me. The water tank exploded that very second. I later saw that the water had landed on the page I was reading. When I returned, I saw that a huge concrete pillar lay across where I'd been sitting. I had heard the very voice of Almighty God – and He saved my life.

I'll jump through to my call to ministry. As I was a Church of Christ member, the nearest training college was in Sydney. When I travelled down by train, I had barely enough money to take me to Sydney. Arriving at Circular Quay, I didn't know how to get to Woolwich Theological College. It was peak hour and the crowds were dense and moving quickly. I prayed, "Lord, get me to college, please."

Through the thick crowd, one young man came forward and asked, "Are you going to Woolwich College?"

"Yes."

"Do you know how to get there?"

"No."

"I'm a student of the college and am going there right now. Can I assist you with your luggage?" The required ferry was the other end of the long line of jetties at Circular Quay.

So I worked my way through college with lawn mowing, gardening, odd jobs, babysitting, and a weekly travelling allowance of two pounds by the church where I was youth pastor. Only three times did I not have the required money for my accommodation and education. On all three occasions, God gave me the exact money to the penny on the last day. That is when you know that there is a God and that you are privileged to serve Him.

In my first year at theological college I was a youth pastor under the leadership of a gentle pastor. I preached vividly on "hell". The next Sunday, with the senior youth group in a circle, pretty Blanche said: "I dreamed about you last night...(cheers all around)... It was a nightmare... (laughter all around)... You were preaching... (a roar of laughter)."

On my last night at the church, the senior youth group were at a 21st birthday party. A shy Alan recognized that it was now or never. Rosemary just 'happened' to be alongside me. My hand reached down and gently held hers. It held back. My romantic skills were about 1 out of 100. The conversation went: "The Balgowlah Church of Christ closed today. I'm restarting the church tomorrow. Would you like to help me?" How did I get such a winner of a wife?

During my last year at college, several churches made approaches to me to become their pastor, but I felt that God was saying "No" each time. On the final day of the college year, Geraldton Church of Christ invited me to become their pastor – and God indicated very clearly that this was the one.

One week later, Rosemary and I married and were soon driving across Australia to Western Australia. Geraldton Church of Christ is where I learned ministry the hard way. At the beginning of our second year at the church, Rosemary said, "I'm so obviously pregnant, you need to take over teaching Grade 1 in Religious Education." On my first day, one child asked if she could go to the toilet. I gave her permission. Fifteen minutes later, the only children in my class were those who had returned from the toilet!

When I told Rosemary the problem, my teacher wife, who was an early childhood specialist, explained, "You stop that problem by saying, 'Only one at a time.'"

Next week, armed with this information, I waited for the first child to raise his/her hand. "May I go to the toilet?" a little girl asked with a raised hand.

"Yes."

It didn't take long for the next person: "May I go to the toilet?" asked a little boy. "Only one person goes to the toilet at a time. You must wait until the girl comes back."

Another girl explained for my benefit, "But they go to different toilets, sir."

By the grace of God alone the church doubled in our three years there.

From there I moved to Bible Society. At a deputation meeting in an Eastern wheatfields town, a traffic cop approached me. "Please help us. Our two ministers can only preach about their doubts about the Christian faith and give no positive message from the Bible." I couldn't see how I could do this, but I promised that I would try.

About two years later, I was pastoring a church three hours away from his town. I'd been given a list of conversions in a crusade that had been conducted in that town several years earlier. But I was on such a low salary, I didn't have the money to go to the town. When the exact amount needed for the trip was sent by mail anonymously, I phoned the traffic cop. He had forgotten the earlier conversation, but said, "Since that time, I've left the Christian faith, but you'd be welcome to stay at my place overnight."

I began to visit on the Friday. The school vice-principal was in Perth. His wife wasn't at home. The school's girls' principal and her farmer husband were in Adelaide because her father had died. One old lady was in England. And I was convinced that God had led me to come on this Friday and Saturday. I knocked on the door of the last person on my list. When I introduced myself, she just stood there gazing and immobile.

Eventually, she invited me in. "I'm sorry. Since my husband died, I have kept asking the two ministers to visit me to help me recover from my grief, but they haven't come. This morning I prayed, "God, if you're there, send me one of your servants today, or I'll know that You're not there. And He sent you today."During the visit, she recommitted her life to Jesus Christ. She told me of another lady in town who would travel by train to Perth (about three hours away) just to speak to Christians who served in a Christian bookshop. My visit to her led to a promise that she would begin a weekly Bible study with the lady I had just visited.

I returned to the vice-principal's wife. She'd returned home. She responded: "Only a week ago, my husband and I said that we've slipped back badly through lack of fellowship. He was a lecturer in a Bible College in New Zealand." Through her tears, she recommitted her life to Jesus Christ. I returned to the traffic cop's home and shared my experiences with him and his wife. The next day, the vice-principal returned and he too recommitted his life to Jesus Christ.

I returned to the traffic cop's home before leaving town. He said, "Visit the vice-principal for girls and her husband on their farm."

I replied, "But they're in Adelaide.".

"God wanted you here these two days. He will have brought

them back in time." The conversation continued about several rounds of repeating ourselves, when he, the non-believer, said to me, the believer: "If you don't phone, I will." The phone kept ringing, and then a lady's voice said, "Hello." I went around to their farm and they told their story. They couldn't obtain a flight from Perth to Adelaide. The best that they could get was Perth to Melbourne to Adelaide. But they knew that that would be too late.

The plane appeared to be preparing for landing well before schedule. The pilot explained: "We've just received a threat that we believe is a hoax. A bomb is supposed to be in the luggage compartment. We are landing in Adelaide." My new acquaintances went immediately to the hospital. Her dying father asked that she recommit her life to Christ. She did and her husband followed. He died soon after.

On their return home, when they were driving down their driveway, they said to each other, "We've recommitted our lives to Jesus, but how can we find fellowship?" At the moment that her hand grasped their front door handle, the telephone rang. Time demonstrated the complete restoration of the traffic cop and his wife to Christ. Later, they were great supporters of Bible Society during my time in that significant mission.

The people whom I visited began a weekly Bible Study. The lady who had been in England became a regular member of that Bible Study. (I later became her daughter's pastor.) When an Aboriginal Church began in that town about one year later, they joined and helped the fledgling church.

As the years went by, we found ourselves in Baptist Churches in Western Australia and Queensland. Eventually, we returned to WA where I became State Director of Bible Society. Weekly visits to churches of all denominations certainly leads you to focus on the essentials of the Faith. During this time, two doctoral degrees were gained, one in New Testament and another in practical ministry. I was also lecturing in three Theological Colleges. I trained to be an Intentional Interim Minister, which meant that my latest ministries were in churches that had had serious division. I was sent in to heal them and set them back on the road to health and growth. This was one of the joys of my life.

. It was during that time that I pastored "the church in the potato field", the Tenthill Baptist Church. It's a small church but, like little children and animals, delightful. When Geoff Cramb wanted me to pastor the church, he knew what I couldn't resist: "Alan, remember the Church of Christ at Chinchilla/Hopelands? Tenthill Baptist is like that." The particular Church of Christ was like moving back into the early church of the New Testament. They loved the Lord Jesus with passion and lived their lives for Him. Tenthill Baptist didn't let Geoff's commendation down. The warmth of their fellowship makes you proud to be a Christian. Their generosity is remarkable. They are the first fruit of a crop. Today, it's always great to go back and share fellowship with them.

Since my retirement, I've been an elder in my local church, while writing two books, both of which are now 90% completed. I've faced death three times after my conversion, including this year, At the edge of death, my response was the same each time, without any thought beforehand as to how I would face it. I just talk to Jesus. "Lord, I didn't have as long to live as I thought, but thank you for the rewarding life you gave me." I know where I'll be going, not because of any good within me, but because I know with absolute certainty that Jesus paid the price for me on Calvary. I have appropriated such an overwhelming privilege. Now I can enter Heaven through His mercy.

11 THE ENGINE JUST STOPPED

The church in the potato field is situated in the middle of the farm operated by Barry Garmeister with the able help of his wife Leone. Barry could be described as a farmer's farmer. He is very, very good at what he does. Barry and Leone's love of and faithfulness towards our church is an example and encouragement to all who worship each week in the potato field.

Back in mid May 1966, a few days before Barry's 18th birthday, the family was involved in the potato harvest. Barry's responsibility was operating and maintaining the potato digger. While his father and brother were having breakfast up in the house, Barry went to grease the harvester which was much easier to do with everything running.

Unfortunately, back in those days little consideration was given to guarding machinery. That day Barry was wearing a new fleecy lined shirt and windcheater and they got caught in a bolt which was part of the rotating machinery. The clothing didn't tear but spun around and wrapped so tight around his neck that it was choking him. Just then, the 55 horsepower tractor, that would happily dig potatoes all day stalled!

Barry's screams for help were heard in the kitchen and, in his haste, Barry's father tripped over the dog and hurt himself but his brother Neville was quickly at the harvester. Grabbing a knife from the shed he cut Barry free from the machinery. He was taken to hospital and kept in overnight. His father came in, looked him over and said, "You will be alright. I am going fishing." And he was alright.

When Reg Crust told his story to me, (the first one in this book), a part I left out was the effect that Barry's mother had on him. She was a praying woman who held devotions with her children every night. We are blessed when we have someone constantly commit our lives to a faithful and capable saviour.

12 THE ENGINE STOPPED AGAIN

They say lightning cannot strike in the same place twice but this account of how Barry and Leone's son, Tony, received lifesaving treatment because, for a second time, an engine wouldn't run, shows that it can. They are blessed to see all their children become committed followers of Jesus.

Sometime around 1980 or 1981 Tony Garmeister was to play the piano at an evening eisteddfod in Lowood, a town about 50 km from Gatton. He had left the family farm at Tenthill feeling well but started to feel very unwell after arriving.

Barry and Leone did not know what to do so they decided to drive home and call in at the Gatton hospital on the way. When Barry pulled up in the car park, Tony said, "I don't feel too bad now." As it was late, his parents then made the reasonable decision to go home and come back in the morning. Just then the hitherto reliable car stopped and refused to start.

Stranded in the car park, the decision was obvious, go in that night and not wait for the morning. It transpired that Tony's appendix was ready to burst and waiting till the morning could have been a disastrous choice. Tony was rushed by ambulance to Toowoomba Base Hospital for an emergency operation.

The next morning Barry was driven into the hospital by his father to try and sort out why the car would not start the night before. On turning the key the engine roared into life and never gave trouble again for the remainder of the time they owned it.

13 WATCHED OVER BY ANGELS

The first chapter, "Follow Me and I will Give You That Farm", tells the story of how Reg Crust found faith in Christ and his service for him along with his wife Heather. This is Heather's own story of her commencement of over forty years' service as a religious instructions teacher in the state schools and how the Lord watched over her in that time. She believes her service was watched over by angels.

Watched over by Angels. This is an awesome thought. I wonder how many times we have been unaware of it. I want to give you just two of the examples that have happened in my life.

But to begin, I want to go back many years and share with you how my passion for religious instruction began. It started when the Lord brought to my attention how I could be of help to my pastor. At that time, Gatton and Tenthill were combined congregations and Pastor Cameron preached at both churches on Sunday morning, as well as a Sunday night service at one of the churches. As well there were all the schools around the area in which he had to teach religious instruction.

I felt the Lord had prepared me. I had taught Sunday School for the little ones in my teenage years and later the young teens. We were living in Mt Sylvia and I felt that, if I offered to teach at our end of the valley, it would help.[9]

Approaching Pastor Cameron after the service one night in Gatton, I offered my help. Pastor Cameron, who was quite deaf, acknowledged my offer but said nothing, I left it at that, feeling I had been obedient to the Lord.

Many months passed when, on one Sunday night, Pastor Cameron came to me and handed me an envelope. On opening it, I found it contained the permission form from the Department of

---

9 It is at least a 20 minute drive from the manse to the Mount Sylvia school.

Education enabling me to teach Religious Instructions in the state schools. As well I had been enrolled in a six week course at the Mount Gravatt Institute of Advanced Education. At that time religious instruction was in transition from being the role of the pastor to the work of lay people. Dr Munday, a lecturer of the college, realised religious instruction teachers needed help in the methods of teaching.

So, for the next six weeks, we travelled to Mt Gravatt. The last two sessions were taken up by us students, having to give a lesson in front of our peers. It was also videoed and played back and then analysed - good and bad. Daunting yes, but I learned so much in preparing and doing a lesson.

Thus I began teaching at Mount Sylvia and Tenthill Upper Schools. (I must admit, I was so nervous in my first lesson. I talked so fast, I was all through in 20 minutes.) However, the number of schools soon reached at least six each week.

Of course, there was the yearly religious instruction or religious education camp as it was affectionately known, which brought in the harvest of the year, such a joy to see so many children coming to believe in Jesus. I guess I could write a book just on that activity. Maybe if the Lord directs.

Going back to the beginning of "angels watching over me", driving to and from schools was part of each day and I want to share just two happenings. Both have involved leaving Mount Whitestone School. I guess it wouldn't happen today as I travel with a mobile phone.

l had just left the school when it was obvious that something was amiss in the car. I coasted to a stop and sat there wondering what to do. That's when I noticed a man wearing overalls, tending his tomato crop. His English was very broad, but he lifted the bonnet, peered in and with his small multi-grips (which he had in his hand), joined the accelerator cable which had snapped and said, "Now that will get you home." And it did and to the mechanic next day.

The second one, once again on leaving Mount Whitestone, I stopped to use the phone at the Ma Ma Creek shop as, being a farmer's wife, I had to call the farm to see if I had to continue on to Gatton to pick up a needed part. When I came out of the phone box, there was a man standing near the car and he said to me, "Lady, you have a flat tyre and, if you have a jack, I will change it for you." And he did. It was the only time in all my driving that I had a flat tyre.

Psalm 91: 11-12. For He will give His angels charge concerning you, to guard you in all your ways. They will bear you up in their hands, lest you strike your foot against a stone.

14 PRAY FOR YOUR HUSBAND

This account of the Good Lord's care comes from Leona Davis, one of the widows of our church. She and her husband Keith were dairy farmers at Carpendale.[10]

During 1988 my husband Keith was engaged in driving cattle to the Grantham abattoir in a semi-trailer.[11] One night, I was woken by an audible voice which said, "Pray for your husband." Keith was away that night with a load of cattle.

I later learnt what happened at the time I was woken. When going down a very steep hill in very heavy rain, the headlights of the truck failed completely. The truck was stopped in the worst possible position and, as well, it couldn't be seen by others. Nor could my husband see where he was going if he proceeded.

Fortunately, a friend was in the truck with Keith and he happened to have a torch. He was able to walk in front of the truck and guide Keith to safety at the bottom of the hill.

---

10 A farming area between Grantham and Helidon in Queensland

11 That is more difficult than general driving as the loads can shift during the trip.

15 IT RAINED FOR 40 DAYS AND 40 NIGHTS

This account by Karen Goodwin tells of the Lord's provision after her home was severely flood affected Prior to January 2011, I would have said that our blessed Lockyer Valley was virtually immune to natural disasters. A few places did flood but there was always plenty of warning. Everything changed on the 10th January 2011 when weeks of almost daily rain was topped off by a very heavy deluge falling on totally saturated soil. In all 19 people in the shire perished from the resulting flooding. A number of communities in our valley were affected but the worst was Grantham which was hit by an "inland tsunami". What happened that day had not been recorded in Australian history and I hope will not be seen again.

So extreme was this devastation that the community was visited by Prince William and our Governor General. The government's response was incredible and virtually everyone who was flood affected was able to move to a new town located on nearby high ground. So also was the nationwide outpouring of compassion.

I was living in Japan teaching English in January 2010 when I was called to the principal's office (never a good thing). The principal, who spoke no English, asked me how I was. Unsure of what he meant, I said in Japanese that I was good. He explained that there had been a *daicozue*, a big flood in Australia to which I replied that Australia was a big place. He pulled my file and pointed to my address, Grantham, and I nodded. When I got home I watched Japanese TV and saw what he meant.

My father contacted me and advised that there was no point returning as there was nothing I could do. (The flood waters had come about 1.7m into the house which itself was 0.9 m above the ground on stumps). So, when the contract finished in March, I came home to witness the aftermath. This is when I saw God's work in helping to rebuild my home.

For eleven days, Grantham was declared a crime scene while the police and armed forces searched for bodies and cleaned up. This meant that locals, who were in an evacuation centre, could not see the true devastation and only sanitised images were released, On the twelfth day, my friends who were in the rural fire brigade, came and fire hosed the house to get rid of most of the silt and debris. My parents worked tirelessly to get rid of my soiled and damaged belongings (furniture etc.), scrubbing walls and sifting through mud for any personal items. A man called John was a welcome visitor to Grantham delivering sandwiches and coffee, tea or fresh water to anyone he could see working on their properties.

When I arrived home in March, my house was clean but it was just a shell with external walls only and with a lot of work and expense required inside and in the yard before I had a home again. My first outside (not family or friends) help came when a group of prisoners arrived and cut down trees and cleared debris. A couple who were touring Australia called in and asked if there was anything they could do so, for 4 ½ hours, they pulled staples out of the kitchen floor. Under multiple layers of lino was a lovely hardwood floor.

My insurance claim came through quickly, after only six weeks, when others waited a year or more, But the payout would not allow me to move my home to the high ground and fit it out as well so I decided to stay. The home is only affected in extreme events and the last one prior to 2011 was in 1974 and then 1893 before that. We hired a builder and he had just finished putting up the VJ pine lining boards when I had a phone call from the recovery centre asking if I was ready for painters? On the following weekend 30 youth and two youth pastors arrived on my doorstep with paint, paint trays and paint brushes. The home was painted inside and out completely at no cost to me.

I received more money from the Premier's Trust and used this to go to Bunnings[12] to purchase the items needed to fit out the house. It had no bathroom, kitchen or floor coverings. Everything was flatpack. Two days after the Bunnings delivery, the Gatton Baptist Pastor rang and said that 25 tradies and wives from a Baptist Church in Adelaide[13] were volunteering their services and could I use help! In ten days my kitchen, bathroom, lighting, plumbing and electrical work was completed. During these ten days they converged at my home for lunch and prayer which was a real blessing in itself. One week later the carpets were laid and on August 6th I moved into the unfurnished house.

My parents were at the recovery centre when a phone call came from someone who had furniture to donate. When he took the call they both recognised each other's voice. It was Noel Wilcox, a former pastor of Tenthill Baptist Church, the church I was attending when I first became a Christian.

---

12 A big box hardware store chain.

13 About 2000 k each way.

16 I THANK GOD FOR MY HUSBAND

Eric and Narelle Couchman are relative new to TenthHill, retiring to the Valley from Northern New South Wales. Eric was a farmer and Narelle a nurse. Eric would be killed in a traffic accident in 2021.

I grew up in the 1950's, one of five children and was blessed to be part of a loving family. We grew up knowing about Jesus and I feel he was always in my life. I met Eric in 1994 and married in 1996. Eric was a widower and had two children from his first marriage and I am blessed that they are now part of my family. We have three granddaughters and two grandsons.

I am writing my Testimony on the theme of the poem "FOOTPRINTS" and how the Lord has impacted my life at certain times. Last year Eric bought me a ring based on Footprints. On the top is a cross that reminds me that Jesus died not only for me but all and our sins are forgiven. Leading up to the cross are the footprints that tell me that Jesus is with us at all times. But in times of need, he carries us.

I have had several experiences over the years where I really felt the Lord's presence. In 1990, my dad passed away at the young age of sixty-three. I didn't know where dad stood in knowing the Lord. He always encouraged us to go to church and Sunday school. Before he passed away, he attended church with mum and allowed the laying on of hands and prayers and visits from the clergy. A few months after he had passed away, I had dream and saw his happy face and he was with his best friend Ted. They told me that they were happy. It took me a long time to know that this was a dream from the Lord and that dad had committed his life to the Lord.

Twice when I had surgery (gall bladder and pancreas), I felt at peace and had no fear. Mum was worried when I had my pancreas operation that I may have had cancer but that thought never entered my head. The Lord has also healed me from breast cancer.

After we married, we lived between Casino and Tenterfield, in northern New South Wales. I worked at a small country hospital 25 km from home. One night, coming home at eleven O'clock, there was a thick fog and I hit something, It was a big bull . I didn't know what damage had been done. I decided to walk back to a house where I had seen lights on. As I was walking down the road I prayed, "PLEASE GOD HELP ME." Right at that moment, a car came down the road and stopped. I could smell alcohol but I had no fear. This young man asked where I lived and he said that he knew our neighbours and he took me home to Eric. This man also went back to the patrol and stayed until we got back there. Then he went home and phoned the NRMA.[14] I never found where he lived to thank him. I really did feel the Lord's presence that night. I thank God for that help as I felt isolated.

These are just a few stories where I felt that the Lord has carried me in my times of trouble. Since I met Eric, I have learnt so much more about our Lord and Saviour. I am truly blessed to have met

---

14 The automobile club in New South Wales.

and married a wonderful Christian man. Thank you Lord for being in my life and bringing Eric into my life and all the blessings you give us.

17 NINE MONTHS TURNED INTO NINE YEARS

Noel Wilcox was an electrical fitter and mechanic before becoming a Christian at Gympie Church of Christ. He met his wife Bev, the daughter of missionary parents there. In 1981, Noel became the first sole pastor for Tenthill, which, prior to that, was shared with Gatton Baptist. Two of their three children were born during their time with us. Noel is, at the time of writing, the pastor of Highfields Baptist Church.

As we were leaving our home church, Gympie Baptist to train at the Baptist Theological College of Queensland (BTCQ) for missionary service, the secretary of the church, Drummond Agnew, quipped, 'I don't believe you should be training for the mission field, but for pastoral ministry' or similar words. My response was, 'Not this kid.'

Bev and I headed off to BTCQ in 1979 while I studied for two years of theological studies. During that time we moved through the interview and application process for missionary service with

Overseas Missionary Fellowship (OMF) in Thailand.

Ormand Porter, the Queensland Secretary for OMF was very helpful in this process. After we had finished at BTCQ, the mission decided we needed more exposure in the area of evangelism. In consultation with the General Superintendent of the Baptist Union of Queensland, Roy Conwell, Tenthill Baptist Church was recommended.

Tenthill graciously accepted this young couple (with their two young children in tow) for a nine month interim in preparation for missionary service. The church was a very mission minded church.

At the end of our intended tenure at Tenthill, Ormand Porter had the unenviable task of informing us that the International Board did not accept our application on medical and psychological grounds. We had been accepted by the State and National Boards of OMF.

When we received the news, Bev said, 'Good. We can have another baby!' We also felt, as did Tenthill, that our work at the church was not complete. It was to be another nine years before we handed over the baton to Peter and Rae Smith.

The Tenthill Church had forged the foundations for a ministry that has now spanned three and a half decades. God had blessed us and the Church in the decade we spent with His faithful servants of Jesus Christ there.

In 1991, our little family had grown to six, four children and their parents.

Our transition from a conservative church with all marriages intact to Bowen, North Queensland where only a handful of marriages were together, was a huge adjustment.

After nine years of ministry in Bowen, strange things began to happen to my body of which we had no knowledge. As time wore on Bev could no longer cope with my condition so I was hospitalised in the Townsville Base Hospital as a psychiatric patient. By the time I was admitted, I was quite psychotic and depressed.

While I was in hospital Bev stayed with Pastor Rudy Behrens and his wife Margaret. Rudy trudged up the hill to the hospital every day, bar two, when his prosthesis caused him too much pain to walk. He assured me God would have me back on pastoral ministry which, in my depressed state, I could not accept.

In the hospital, while on the highest doses of antidepressants and anti-psychotics, there was no improvement. My pleas, that this was a spiritual problem, fell in deaf ears.

After being 'interred' in the psychiatric ward for three weeks, the professionals consulted one another and agreed electric shock therapy was the next option. It was scheduled for the Monday morning. Bev was devastated.

Unbeknown to Bev, on the Friday night Rudy and Margaret Behrens had organised a prayer meeting. Meanwhile, at the hospital, I had decided I would not leave my knees in prayer, even 'if I had to stay all night.' By the way, I was unaware of the intended treatment for the Monday, but I had spoken to another patient who was undergoing the treatment.

While on my knees, God revealed the source of my problem, which I confessed and things began to change. Meanwhile back at the Behrens household, Margaret greeted Bev with 'Noel is okay; we have prayed through. Saturday morning, Bev could not believe what she saw. Her husband was smiling for the first time in probably six months.

Recovery from that point was slow. Three months rehabilitation after which the Bowen church graciously allowed us to minister again, part time. It was not until about two years had passed before most of the healing had finished its process.

The turn-around in hospital was nothing short of a miracle and one for which we praise God from the depth of our hearts for His act of grace.

18 STANLY WASN'T READY FOR HEAVEN

What can I say about Stanley. Stanley is special and a good friend. Stan has worked as a chef and a boner in an abattoir and, as a mature age student, completed a dual degree in biosecurity. Poor health means he is now unemployed and knows what it is like to seek the Lord daily for his needs. Stan organises some very special meals for our monthly fellowship tea.

I was 26 and living with my parents in Mt. Garnet[15] and, around my birthday, my friend David came over about 8 am in the morning in his Suzuki soft top 4WD. David and I discussed where to go for my birthday and we decided on the Irvinebank pub. Irvinebank is a small village about 40 kilometres away.

We took the back road from Mt Garnet to Irvinebank which was a dirt track. After having a few beers at the pub, my friend David asked me to drive on the way back. I replied that I had had too

---

15 Mt Garnet is situated on the Atherton Tableland and is about a three hour drive north-west of Cairns.

many beers and I would prefer not to drive. He said, "I will drive then." David then took off at high speed and, only 200 metres down the road, drove straight over the side of the Irvinebank bridge after hitting the kerb. The force of the impact threw David, his dog and myself out of the Suzuki. The vehicle ended upside down in the creek that had about 900 mm of water in it. If we had our seat belts on we would have drowned.

The force of the impact threw me about 20 metres into a tree about five metres up hitting it with the left side of my body. This resulted in a branch going into my leg and another branch went through my ear and penetrated my skull narrowly missing my brain. I felt every branch as I fell to the ground. I was knocked unconscious. Part of me left my body and I was looking down at myself lying there lifeless. I was aware that I was ascending while still watching my body. I entered a passageway with a very faint light. The whole passage was enveloped with large white glazed tiles. The white tiles then turned into angels' wings and they were leading me up what was now a round tunnel to the light. As the wings got bigger, the breeze from their flapping wings was pushing me along. The light got very large and I felt myself touching the light with my body. As I felt myself going into the light, a feeling of euphoria came over me and I felt total peace and tranquillity. While this was happening I heard loud music from a large pipe organ similar to a cathedral.

I heard three voices, two female, one male, telling me not to be scared to come into the light. I felt they were relatives that had passed on. I then prayed to God and told him I wasn't ready to go and that my work on Earth wasn't done. All of a sudden, I was back in my body wracked in pain but totally sober. I opened my eyes to see a beautiful woman standing over me. She looked like an angel, but who just happened to live in a house near the creek. She reached into her pocket and brought out an embroidered handkerchief and placed it on my head to stop a small cut that had covered my whole forehead with blood. She then asked if I was alright. I said that I have some concussion and asked how my friend and the dog were. When I went to stand up I felt shooting pains from my knees and the front of my thighs from where I had been catapulted out of the vehicle.

She got us some help from a nurse that worked at Herberton hospital[16] and we stayed overnight at the nurse's house. She fed us and washed my wounds. After conferring with a doctor, she didn't think it was urgent that we went to hospital.

During the night I couldn't sleep because I was in pain. Due to the stress of the accident, it felt as if someone was trying to punch me in the head. As the vehicle wasn't driveable my parents were informed about the accident and came the next day to pick up David, the dog and myself. They took us to Herberton hospital where I was assessed by the local doctor who said, "You are a very lucky man as the branch missed your brain by six millimetres." We then drove home.

At that time my parents were Jehovah's Witnesses and I was brought up in that faith. Six month after the accident I moved back to Toowoomba and met *A Fellowship of Christians* and came to faith.

---

16 About an hour's drive on the way to Cairns

19 WE ARE NOT DONE YET

This account is the story of David and Barbara Leek's journey to (and with) Tenthill Baptist fellowship. The account is in Barbara's words.

We were married in 1968 and lived in the suburbs of Sydney but after the birth of our two daughters, Teresa and Sharron, we both felt it would be better to raise our family in the country and not in the city.

We looked at various options, motels, caravan parks, small businesses but nothing was forthcoming. So we almost resigned to forget about this dream. After about six months, one Saturday morning, David announced he was going to buy the paper and have another look. He found an advertisement for a small engineering business in the beautiful Lockyer Valley in Queensland. We had no idea where this was so, after looking in the post code book, we found that 4343 was Gatton. With David being a fitter and turner/toolmaker, this seemed too good to be true. After coming up and looking at the business we made an offer and went back down south to sell our house. Twelve months later, we left our home, family and friends and came to live at Caffey[17]. This was June, 1973.

We had made a decision that the very first Sunday we would go to church. We had arrived on the Thursday so we drove to town to see where that would be. But on the way I told David to go back. I had noticed a faded sign which read "Tenthill Baptist Church". We were amazed that we didn't even have to drive into town. The Lord had shown us where we were to fellowship!

My father moved up with us to help with the business (my mother came a couple of months later). So on that first Sunday, we left our two girls with him and went to church. Teresa was three and Sharron was 18 months old and being from the city and naïve we thought that the church would probably be older folk and having two little ones this might not have been a good idea...wrong! We were in the company of many around our own age and there were lots of children. We were so full of praise that the Lord had led us to this small country church.

We arrived in a Rambler[18] station wagon with black and yellow number plates[19] so there were many who thought we were just seasonal workers. It took some time before the fellowship realised we were permanently in the area. On that first Sunday, the first person to speak to us was Dawn Windolf.[20]

Three years later in 1976 our 'genuine Queenslander" Jennifer was

---

17 A few kilometres further up the Tenthill valley.

18 A vehicle from American Motors Corporation. It ceased production in the US in 1969 but continued in Australia til 1983.

19 Queensland plates were black and white so the plate stood out.

20 Her outstanding lemon meringue pies get a mention in my book Sermons from a Potato Field.

born and this made our family complete.

David spent time teaching Sunday school and I was a member of the Tenthill Ladies' Choir. Singing with these sisters in Christ was a privilege and a wonderful blessing. We travelled to many different churches presenting a program in song and music, finishing with Ula Binggeli using her talent with a relevant sketch/drawing.

We were involved in the weekly Bible study in the Mt Sylvia area, going to the homes of Reg and Heather Crust, Keith and Joan Dorr and Albert and Ula Binggeli. These folk helped us so much on our spiritual journey, along with the encouragement and teaching from the pastors who have led the fellowship.

When John Biggs was our pastor we were both baptised and became members. We were the last to be baptised in the old corrugated iron baptistery It needed to be replaced and the story went around it was replaced because there were too many 'Leeks' in it!

David was nominated and elected as a Deacon and a few years later when Elders were introduced, he was nominated and elected to be part of that team.

We were asked to accompany Doug Ensby, who was the youth director, on a youth camp and, not long after, when Doug left to go to Bible college, David was appointed the youth director.

This was the start of a different journey. We had a decision to make, so we advertised the business at Caffey (in the Sydney paper) and received a reply from Brian and Diane Greenham. When they arrived to see what we had for sale, we were sitting around the table and Diane asked us, "Where is the closest church?" Two weeks later, the business was sold and our journey with the youth ministry began. Once again the Lord was guiding our path and answering our prayers. Brian and Diane and their family became part of our fellowship at Tenthill.

Our business and our home was sold so we moved into our current home (which we were building and was not finished) and David continued working on a smaller scale in 'his shed'.

We spent many years with the youth group, and still to this day our love for young people has not left us. We have lots of precious memories and many special friends. We have come across folk who were involved in our 60 plus youth group, who remember us, but it has been hard sometimes to recognise them.

We started a Tuesday night dinner and Bible study in our home with the young people and this is still going. Spaghetti bolognaise was the meal we provided and one night we had more than the usual number arrive. I commented to David that I was worried there wouldn't be enough, but, after everyone had been served there was still plenty left over. Praise the Lord.

We had many wonderful youth leaders to take care of the Friday night youth group and so for three years we had 'Jacob's Well coffee shop' in the CWA[21] hall in Gatton every Friday night, witnessing on the streets of Gatton, inviting folk to come for coffee and a chat. Many of the young people came in after youth group. It was during this time we arranged the "Jesus Youth Fest" music event at the shire hall which ran for three years.

As part of the youth ministry we had the opportunity to go on short term mission trips. Several to Kalkaringi[22] in the Northern Territory and a wonderful overseas trip to Manila in the Philippines, and we will never forget the great times when the young people were involved in the musicals, 'Bow Down' and

21 Country\Women's Association
22 A very remote community.

'Waiters'. Also all the youth camps and youth exchange weekends. We were blessed to have a fellowship that encouraged and helped us with the youth ministry.

Our three daughters were all baptised and married at Tenthill. (Teresa married Stewart Pieper[23]. Sharron married Paul Windolf and Jennifer married Tony Johnston (Stewart and Paul's cousin).

Now in our 'senior years', we are so grateful for our time at Tenthill, the youth work, the choir, the eldership team, the craft group and now with our new line dancing crew! We love the saying from Bill Hybels, "If you are not dead you are not done!" So, with our Lord's grace and direction we will continue on this journey with the fellowship at Tent Hill Baptist.

---

23 At the time of writing, Stewart is the Acting General Superintendent of Queensland Baptists

20 GREAT IS THY FAITHFULNESS

At the time of writing, Chris Meyer is an elder at Tenthill Baptist Church and he, along with his wife Georgi, head up the music ministry. Chris and Georgie both work at Emu Gully Adventure Camp where all activities are focussed on the core character values of Courage, Mateship, Perseverance and Sacrifice. Chris's sermon, The Parable of Hank, is found in my book "Sermons from a Potato Field".

Things were getting desperate. My wife Georgi and I had just completed Bible College the year before which had exhausted our finances. We felt the Lord calling us back to the rodeo scene to minister to the elite world of the professional rodeo cowboy. I had started competing again in the saddle bronc (riding bucking horses) event at the beginning of the year and, by May, I was ranked second in the country.

We had also just been accepted by Athletes in Action, a sports' ministry under Campus Crusade for Christ. At the time, we were still raising our support team and funds were pretty tight. A few months earlier, we had gone to a rodeo at Kyabram and the F100 ambulance that was being used there was for sale. A few days later I was telling a friend about it and how it would really suit our ministry needs but that I would have to sell our car first. He graciously offered to pay for the F100 and was happy for us to pay him back when we sold our car.

This all seemed pretty straight forward except that we hadn't been able to sell our car. We had organized a ministry trip to coincide with the "Northern run", a circuit of rodeos that went through Queensland up to Darwin and back down the east coast of Australia. We were to speak at two Scripture Union camps at Wandoan and Blackall in the school holidays and had organized a host of speaking engagements from men's breakfasts, youth groups and churches to primary and secondary schools in the towns we would be travelling through while competing at rodeos.

There was one small problem - we had no idea how we were going to fund this expedition as we didn't have enough money to make it past the front gate. A campsite down in Victoria had kindly given us a house to come and go as we pleased with the proviso that I would work there when I was available. It was an amazing provision especially since we had two small children at the time and gave them some stability when we weren't on the road in the caravan. I remember getting introduced once as the man with no fixed address but such is the life of a travelling cowboy.

It was Wednesday morning, middle of June and we were to leave on the Friday to go to Tapio rodeo on the Victorian/New South Wales border on our way to Wandoan in Queensland and the Northern run of rodeos. Things were desperate. We still hadn't sold the car, no money for fuel or entry fees let alone food etc. I got up about 5 am to light the fire and spend some time with the Lord before heading over to the camp to start breakfast for the campers. As I began to explain our predicament to the Lord I was reminded of an old hymn "Great is Thy Faithfulness". In the stillness I began to sing the words.

"Great is Thy faithfulness,
Great is Thy faithfulness,
Morning by morning new mercies I see.
All I have needed thy hands hath provided.
Great is Thy faithfulness, Lord unto me."

As I sang this song the presence of the One who is faithful, the LORD Almighty filled the room and enveloped me. Tears streamed uncontrollably as the Holy Spirit put his hand on my shoulder and peace flooded my being. When I finally rose and left the house I knew everything would work out.

That night as I walked in the door I was met by a very excited Georgi. She told me how a guy came, had a look at the car, said it was exactly what he wanted and bought it. He paid the specific amount we needed for the F100. Another lady called in. She had been in a church where I preached the previous Sunday night. She told Georgi how the Lord had spoken to her and her husband (who were both teachers) through my message to leave their home town and move to Queensland to serve the Lord in a Christian school there. She also gave Georgi a gift of $500. That was enough to buy all the stuff we needed for our trip and get us to Tapio. I won the bronc ride there which got us to the next leg of the trip.

We arrived back in Victoria five months later overwhelmed by our Heavenly Fathers amazing provision. We had travelled the length and half the breadth of this country and everywhere in between and we had never once gone without. We saw kids give their lives to Christ on camps including the volunteer cook at Blackall. We preached to thousands of people and saw lives changed for eternity as well as being salt and light on the rodeo circuit. I don't know how we did it. I can't explain it. I imagine it felt a bit like Peter walking on water. We were completely relying on Jesus. And we found Him to be truly faithful.

21 GIVING THANKS

Ula Binggeli along with her husband Albert became members of Tenthill Baptist Church in the 1950's. Albert passed to his well-earned reward in 2010. Ula has not had an easy life and hard work took a toll on her body and, as a consequence, has endured many years of pain. Somewhere in a busy life, Ula developed a love and a skill for painting and has been holding art classes for many years. She is held in such high regard in our community that she was recognised as the Lockyer Valley Regional Council's senior cultural award in 2007 and given the Mayoral Award in 2017 In the image, Ula is looking at the Concordia Lutheran college students registration book with her painting of Albert in the background.

The mayor said when presenting her award that Ula "significantly improves the lives of both individuals and the community and contributes to the Valley's vision of a region built on strength and diversity. [She] is held in very high esteem in the local and wider community."

I had a very unsettled family life as my parents did not get along which, consequently, saw me living in Cooranga North, Maroochydore, Mt Larcom, Hervey Bay and My Sylvia. Later I commenced nursing in Gatton Hospital and met Albert during this time. His family had migrated from Switzerland in 1928 and settled on a share farm at East Haldon.[24] Life was very hard for them and Albert's father would walk every weekend over the mountains to work on the huge cutting engineered by Theiss Brothers.[25] This meant Albert missed some schooling because he had to do the farm work though, later, Pastor Koehler assisted him. (He rode a horse up the valley from the Lutheran Church at Ropely to minister to people who lived "up the creek".) There were 13 creek crossings from Gatton to our place. Through his encouragement (and possibly payment due to his parent's poverty) he became the first student at Concordia Lutheran College.

I married Albert when I was 18 years of age and settled on the farm and his parents moved to Wynnum. We were dairy farmers at that time which meant early to rise at 4 AM each morning to get the milking done and the cream out to the road for the cream carter to collect and take to the Grantham Butter Factory. We milked twice a day with our three children safely in a large wooden container. Problems arose when Russell became a climber and we had to chain his belt to the box. We had no electricity or vehicle for 10 years. I would go into town with Harry Kerr's delivery truck amid the bread and meat boxes. Returning, everyone got their unwrapped bread put on top of their gate post and the sugar bag with meat hung on the fence. This was an all-day affair with a long stop at the Tenthill pub. The creek crossings between Gatton and our place always had water over them. Cement crossings came much later.

---

24 At the top end of our valley, a long way from the Tenthill church

25 The cutting at Mt Whitestone is a local landmark, the company went on to be a major firm in Queensland. The walk was 8km as the crow flies over some of our steepest hills, many times longer using the roads.

Unless you have lived "up the creek" you cannot understand how restrictive it was as in those days as the creek was always running and the creek ruled your life. I remember water running through the car and bagging the engine at every crossing and then, once, for three months unable to get to town as all the crossings were washed away.

I was by birth a Seventh Day Adventist and Albert was Lutheran, but the family were not church goers at that time. I had nursed George Dorr[26] in hospital and knew the family. Thanks be to God; George had his son Keith drive up to our place and take the children and me to Tenthill church and Sunday school. (There was no room for Albert in the car.) That was a wonderful gesture considering the unsealed roads and creek crossings. Later when we were able to purchase an old car Albert was able to join us.

Harry Castle[27] was doing some rotary hoeing at our farm the night before the Billy Graham crusade and he asked if we would like to go with him to Brisbane. We drove down and the effect it had on Albert was terrific, but he did not go forward though after that he listened to religious programmes on the radio on Sunday evening (Lutheran Hour, Back to the Bible). One day he met our pastor, Percy Walters, in town and asked if he would talk to us about God. Percy came up that night and he was very good at teaching us. When there was a crusade in Toowoomba in 1959, Albert came forward. Albert, Susan and Philip were all baptised at Tenthill. Russel and I were baptised in Brisbane.

After George Dorr died, a lifelong friendship grew between Keith and Joan and Albert and me. The Tenthill Baptist Church became our spiritual home and for me still is. Good and wonderful friendships emerged into my lonely life. To mention Dawn and

---

26 We have seen four generations of the Dorr's as members of our church.

27 Harry is a very faithful Anglican who for many decades taught religious education in the schools

John Windolf[28] who ministered on many occasions and were close friends to us. Joan and Wilf Neuendorf became a big part of our lives with our picnics on the creek bank enjoying together the beauty of God's creation. These would continue on to include a tea meal before going home. Their friendship lasted till they died. Joan was always there to pray for me personally or on the phone after Albert died. We were blessed by wonderful home prayer meetings that lasted for years. This meant a lot to us. The Tenthill Ladies Choir lasted for many years where we gave programmes from Brisbane to Stanthorpe and all in between and a senior citizens programmes. Tenthill church was and is a great place to worship our Lord. I want to honour Tenthill Baptist Church and the people in it for assisting my family in our spiritual walk.

---

28 Four generations of the Windolf's have been associated with Tenthill Baptist Church.

22 RESTORATION IN THE POTATO PATCH

This testimony is from Tim Grant, who for six and a half years was employed as the Youth Pastor of Tenthill Baptist Church. His engagement in this role was beyond our offerings at the time but we were convinced that this was what the Lord wanted and the funds became available. His ministry was blessed and flourished when he had to stand in as the pastor after Pastor Russell resigned. He was ably assisted by his wife Vanessa. Tim left Tenthill to become the senior pastor at Mt Isa Baptist Church in 2019. We were blessed to have them as our own for this time.

We arrived in Tenthill immensely exasperated. We had just served two years of a three-year contract at a church of another denomination as the youth pastor. Our announcement of resignation to the church members and final day at that church were on the same day, the senior and executive pastor were happy to see me leave.

Let me provide some context. We arrived at that church in 2011, shortly before we were married. Although we couldn't put our finger on the cause, the culture of the youth ministry was toxic, they wanted to be cool... but they didn't want Jesus. Several incidents from the leaders highlighted to me the resistance I was up against. During one youth group event, someone had put on a 'Katy Perry' song full of sexual innuendo. I asked the youth to change the music. The leader who had put the song on raced to the sound desk to object!

On another occasion, at a leaders meeting, we were talking about the purpose of our Friday night program. One leader retorted, 'Friday nights are not about telling youth the gospel.'

The church, being driven by growth, wanted to see the youth group grow as well. But no spiritual growth, let alone numerical growth was going to occur with the current state of things.

What was happening?

At the end of our first year, we arrived back from our Christmas holidays. I began making phone calls to families inviting the youth to a school holiday pool event. The first family I called, replied they had let the church, So did the second, and the third. I talked to the executive pastor and received only ambiguous hints at what had happened... inappropriate behaviour from some of the leaders.

So I talked to some other people in the know to find out the details.

The elder's son, (who was previously the youth leader before my arrival) was sleeping with the senior pastor daughter's while dating the worship pastor's daughter and making inappropriate passes at several of the youth girls. Another leader that I had inherited and was the son of a staff member was interfering with teenage girls.

No wonder they didn't want Jesus. Unfortunately for us, the perpetrators were all sons and daughters of the pastors, elders and members of staff. They protected their (adult) children and covered up as much as possible.

A court case followed and one of the leaders received a suspended sentence.

The church leaders still wanted a big youth group. But a turnaround after that bombshell... and the coverups was unlikely.

However, the senior and executive pastor wanted me gone. They did this through an increasing number of service reviews. I was only required to have one per year. In a period of less than one year, the senior and executive pastors tried to drag me through three reviews.

An extract from my letter of complaint penned by a director of HR provides greater context to the situation and my response.

> *As a result of the continuing inappropriate actions of some Church representatives, I must draw to your attention the repeated harassing and bullying behaviour I am experiencing in my employment with [redacted].*

Clearly these actions are designed and focussed on forcing me to resign from my fixed term role and are not reasonable action on the part of the Church through its representatives in regards my employment.

A discussion with [redacted] and [redacted] was held in early October to finalise my belated Service review anticipated for late June or early July 2012. At that meeting, the matters arising from my previous review were discussed and there was general agreement that those items had been positively progressed. There being no negative commentary or follow up in writing to the contrary in the last 2 months, it is fair and reasonable to presume no continuing issues exist. However I am now required to attend another Service Review scheduled for Wednesday 12 December 2012: my third in less than 12 months. I allege that such action is workplace harassment with the sole intent of intimidating, threatening or fabricating a means to terminate my employment.

I make this allegation to yourselves and the Church on the basis of the discussions undertaken by the Senior Pastor with me on at least 3 discussions throughout November 2012 wherein he required a date from me regarding my resignation from my role that has a further 13 months to run before conclusion. Such continuing and repeated discussions on this matter are clearly harassment under the provisions of the Act. I was forced to recently send an email to the Senior and Executive Pastors of this Church to indicate that I would not concede to participating in any further discussions regarding forcing me to resign with the hope that the harassment might End.

Because I have not chosen to bow to such victimisation and unreasonable action of Officers of the Church, I do perceive that the forthcoming Service Review to be another attempt to find a means to terminate my employment. I am comfortable to make this allegation and lodge this complaint with you on the basis that no documentation exists to suggest on-going performance deficiencies or justification for yet another review within a 12 month period.

The actions of representatives on behalf of the Church are clearly focussed on creating a means to end my employment inappropriately, harshly and unjustly. On the basis of my complaint to you, I will not be attending the requested review for which I have received no prior documentation concerning any matters that will be discussed and allege to you as evidence of harassment.

Yours faithfully,

Tim Grant

I was beyond stressed. Not only was I on Zoloft, but my doctor also prescribed Valium to help with the anxiety.

There were, however, some other very good Godly men that made up the rest of the eldership. They called in a workplace investigator to investigate the claims I had made. The investigator found grounds for my complaint. The bullying stopped and one of the elders resigned, appalled that this had happened.

In the meantime, I had begun talking to Pastor Iain Russell at Tenthill Baptist Church. I had more conversations with Iain before I was employed at Tenthill then I had with the senior pastor of my current position in my whole time of employment.

The longest conversation I had with the senior pastor there was when he asked me when I was leaving.

On the 23 December 2012, I received a call to Tenthill Baptist Church. I provided my resignation to my current church, the rest of the members were notified of my resignation and final day on the 30 December 2012, most of them none the wiser as to what had happened. What a relief it was to leave.

To the credit of our previous church, we received an apology several months after we had left.

For six and a half years, we were lovingly embraced by Tenthill Baptist Church, and we embraced them. While none of us were perfect, Vanessa and I gained a little glimpse of heaven through the Godly men and women of this church. I particularly appreciated my relationship with Pastor Iain, who cared for us and cheered us on as we served the youth. Even on those very few occasions we disagreed, or I had done the wrong thing, he still treated me like a Christian brother.

For a period, Ness and I didn't want to return to local church ministry, so we studied to perhaps leave for the mission field. Our passion for local church ministry returned, particularly as we experienced life in a healthy church, with healthy leadership.

We are thankful for the sacrifice that a small country church made to employ a youth pastor, and I think Tenthill has reaped the fruit of that sacrifice, with many young people, (many who have now left the area), continuing to follow Jesus. We are thankful that we were able to play a small part in that fruitfulness.

We are immensely thankful for our time at Tenthill Baptist and immensely thankful for its people. We were able to grow as a couple, have a family, heal from our prior experience and serve as best we could. We would not have had the opportunity to be at this special church if it weren't through God's providential direction of our lives leading us through two very difficult years prior to our arrival.

23 A CALL TO MISSIONS

This chapter tells the story of the call to missions of Lachlan and Tiffany Struthers and was written by Tiffany. Both came through our youth group. Tiffany is the daughter of Chris and Georgie Meyer (See Chapter 20). The decision to start a youth work was beyond our budget at the time but we believed that if it was God' will he would provide. This I part of the fruit of that ministry.

After growing up in a Christian family and attending Tenthill Baptist for many years with my family I decided to commit my life to God at a camp called *Teenstreet* in 2013. I was really challenged with the idea that 'your parents' faith is not your own' and that I had not taken God's will into my own life and had instead been holding him at a distance. The next year, my senior year of high school, I met the man who is now my husband. He was introduced to Jesus at *Teenstreet* in 2014 when my brother invited him to come to this 'really fun' and 'not super Christiany' camp. Of course this description vastly downplayed just how important a place Jesus held in this camp! After a week in a servant leadership role within the camp (because he was in his first year of university and too old to be involved as a participant) and learning not just how to be a servant leader like Jesus, but also learning WHO Jesus is, he decided to give God a chance.

Over the next year Lachlan grew a lot in understanding who God is and came to the realisation of what Jesus did for him on the cross, praise Jesus! The next year at *Teenstreet* I was in my first year of university and this time we were both involved as servant leaders at the camp (called GAP leaders). During that time we each, individually, signed up for a *Teenstreet*-run, two-week mission trip to Nepal and only a few weeks later we started dating. This mission trip to Nepal was a huge step for Lachlan and I as a couple but also as followers of God and in how we viewed missions.

During this time I had the chance to get to know some incredible missionaries, not incredible because of their outstanding faith, memorisation of the entire bible or amazing evangelising abilities as many in the western church view missionaries, but incredible because of the way that they give their flawed lives as lights in the places that they serve. It opened my eyes to the normalcy of mission life, but also the hardships surrounding it. Before this trip I had never even considered overseas missions for myself because of what I now come to believe was a subconscious wrong view of what a missionary was as a person.

My husband, who at the time was still in the middle of his anthropology and history bachelor, had already been thinking about the possibility of overseas mission as a way to serve God with his passions around culture and people groups that he was studying about. On the last day of this mission trip in January of 2016, during our quiet devotion time in the morning, I sought out Lachlan to check in with him about how he was feeling after such an intense few weeks. He told me then that he felt he was called to overseas missions… after a moment's thought I said to him "well, then you will have to marry me first and take me with you!"

Now I tell people that I was really the one to propose to Lachlan! Though he did officially propose to me a few months later and we got married that November. The next year we decided to let OM Australia know about our call to missions. They are responsible for Teenstreet and because, at this point, we had each been impacted so greatly through these camps and been involved for quite a few years in this ministry in differing capacities and roles we knew OM and its vision very well. We didn't think twice that this was the organisation we should go with.

In January 2018, after having some doors close and giving OM our 'resume' we contacted OM Albania to talk about joining their Roma/Gypsy ministry the following January for a two year commitment. It became clear to us that this was the place that God wanted us and so we started the process of applying and getting our documents in order. We had pre-field training at the OM Australia's base in Melbourne in July and a few months later were accepted by OM Albania! Wooh! It was a very exciting day but also meant that we only had about four months to raise our support so that we could start in January. At this time I had just finished my Bachelor of Creative arts and Lachlan was now doing a one year Graduate Diploma in Theology after completing his Bachelor, double majoring in History and Anthropology. So because Lachlan was still studying full time it was mostly up to me!

During that time I was so amazed and encouraged by the way that God worked in our lives for our good and for his glory. For example, one thing I will never forget: We had discovered that we needed 80% of our support to be pledged by the end of November so that we could book flights and register for Go conference before the deadline. We discovered this at the start of November! Only a month and a half into support raising we were at about 25% pledged and it looked completely unattainable. So we called and visited people and churches and continued in our efforts. On the last day we were at 75%!! Which in itself was a miracle in just over 3 weeks. We went to sleep the night before with this 75% not knowing even of possible supporters to contact for the last of our support. The next day, the last possible day before the deadline, we made up the last of our needed support from places and people that we had never thought possible.

If we had been going about support raising with our own strength, our own abilities, we would have been finished. We had no more ideas, no skill in fund raising whatsoever. Without God's hand there is no way we would be in Albania now, serving for His kingdom. To me that was so much more of a confirmation for His calling because if it was not His will, He could have *very easily* closed this door for us. Even though we try to do things in our own strength we can't... but God can do SO MUCH MORE than we could ever imagine.

24 GOD IS PROVIDER

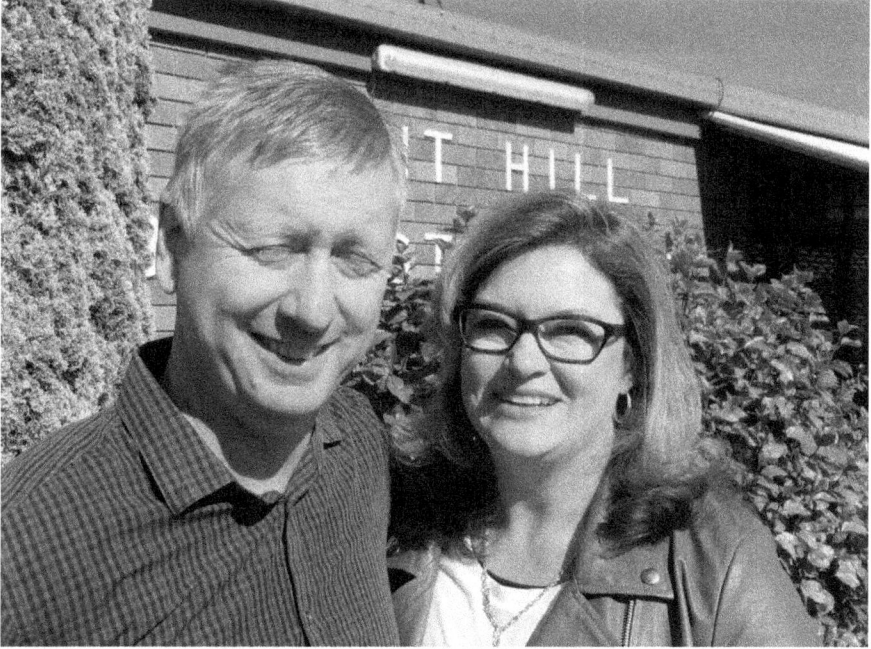

Memories of life from the church in the potato patch by Warren Dorr. For many years he led the music ministry at Tenthill.

There were many instances over the years where it has been evident that God is faithful and provides. Through droughts, floods, crop failures and low prices, God's hand has always provided for our needs.

I was appointed joint youth leader when I was about 19, at a time when there was quite a small Youth group at the church. I remember going to the annual church meeting for the election of leadership positions not having been asked by anyone about standing as leader but just feeling in my heart that this was a position that God would have me take on. I wasn't surprised then when I was nominated and elected as a Youth Leader. I implemented a Games and Bible Study program where we had a fortnightly rotation with Bible studies one week then games and activities with a devotion the next. On my first night as leader, after much prayer we had a huge number of youth attend from all over our district. We soon had up to 60 youth regularly attend the program on Friday nights, with almost equal numbers attending the bible study nights. Many youth were impacted with the Gospel and are continuing to serve God today.

One novel answer to prayer was when our Youth Group was attending a Youth Exchange program (where the youth travelled to Brisbane to connect with a group from another church for a weekend of activities and participating in ministry in church services) when on the way to Brisbane my car stopped on the highway. We got out and prayed then hopped back in the car and it started straight away and ran fine all weekend. At the first opportunity I got after returning home, I booked it into a mechanic. On driving to the mechanic, the car ran terribly and finally stopped just as I turned into the workshop driveway. It was amazing how God kept the car going during the weekend in answer to prayer.

One of my earlier memories of God's provision was in the late 80's when we had a severe drought and we had been struggling for years to keep crops growing. We had become very discouraged. Some rain was finally forecast but is seemed impossible that there would be enough rain to cause the creek to flow in order to replenish our underground water supplies which we used to irrigate our crops. One night, however, the rain started to fall and I spent what seemed like hours pleading with God in prayer that there would be enough rain to cause the creek to flow to fill the underground aquifer. After a considerable amount of time, I just felt a sudden peace come over me and an incredible assurance that God had heard me and was going to answer my prayer and that the next day the creek would be flowing. I fell asleep with a great sense of peace. I remember waking up with excitement the next day and I rushed out of bed fully expecting my mother to greet me with the news that the creek was flowing. I remember saying to her "Isn't the creek flowing" and watching her shake her head. I couldn't believe it as I was so certain that God was going to answer my prayer. I was confused and got some breakfast and sat at the table when we realised that the traffic was slowing as they approached the creek crossing. I jumped up with joy and raced down to the creek to see a nice stream of water flowing. Of course God had answered my prayer.

In another especially severe drought in the late 90's, I remember walking past one of the bores which we relied on for irrigation water. The volume of water we could get from the bore had reduced to just a small amount and I was wondering and praying about how we were going to get by and whether the bore would continue to provide life giving water. I can remember literally hearing the words as if they were spoken out loud "The oil jar will never run dry". This was of course a reference from the Bible story where God was providing for Elijah during an extreme drought where he was staying with a Widow and her son where the only source of food was from a couple of jars of flour and oil that miraculously refilled each day. In like manner the water never completely ran out and we always had enough to get the crops through that we were growing at the time.

At one point, one of the main crops we were growing was Lettuce, which is a very costly crop to grow and one year we were only one day away from harvesting when we had a severe hail storm (which is very uncommon in winter) and upon inspecting the damage the next day it initially appeared that the crop was completely destroyed. We were left bewildered and concerned that a large portion of our yearly income had been wiped out. We committed it to God. The next day we had the crop inspected by the director of the company who looked after the distribution of our produce and to our amazement found that the only the outer leaves had been damaged and the hearts inside were undamaged. A good friend from our church put us in contact with a company that supplied lettuce hearts to a food processing company. An amazing miracle that the soft inner hearts of the lettuce were not damaged and we harvested the entire crop.

Over the years we tried many different crops and even increased the number of cattle we were running to see if we could find a way to keep our family farming business going. It was looking inevitable that we would have to increase our operations further to have a greater turnover of produce to make up for the shrinking profit margins that seemed to be constantly getting smaller. I didn't want to go down the path of obtaining more land and increasing the size of our operations which would only add to the busyness and stress of life, so started we started to think seriously about finding other ways to make a living.

Droughts, however, had seemed to be coming a regular part of life on the farm and another particularly severe drought occurred in the early to mid-2000's which coincided with this time when we were considering our future options. Lorraine, my wife, who was an amazing support through this time, suggested I get some higher qualifications in music and after being encouraged by a couple of friends as well, I applied to do a university degree in music. I figured that it would have to be better teaching music than labouring on other people's farms to supplement our income. The catch was how to farm and study during a drought because of the extra time it seemed to take to even grow the smallest amount of crops. We were doing all sorts of things to try to extract irrigation water from bores that had almost completely depleted. And this was without even considering how we were going to afford to pay study fees and expenses.

I felt led to apply to enrol at University and had to gain entry by audition (I hadn't even completed Grade 11 and 12 at school). I was subsequently successful at getting entry and enrolled as a full time student and payed the fees upfront in order to get discounted fees. It was a miracle in itself that I paid the fees up front for the entire degree and never accrued any HECS debt to the Government for the University course. We had huge debt, however, on some farming property which we had purchased a few years earlier in an attempt to run more cattle as a way of boosting income. We applied for and received drought subsidies that the government was offering at the time to help cover interest on repayments and allowed reskilling and evaluation of a future career. This was an amazing provision of God as our ability to grow crops was drastically reduced due to the extreme shortage of water to irrigate crops. I look back and am just amazed at how God provided for us through that time and that as soon as I stepped out in faith God stepped in and met all of our needs. I was able to keep a trickle of potatoes and cabbage growing alongside studying full time for the first year or so. It was a busy time though, as during these years I had to travel to Brisbane (2 hour drive) once a week for Instrument lessons and Toowoomba twice a week to play in music ensembles as part of my study units as well as everything else I had to do including raising a family.

One Sunday we went with friends of ours to a service at theichurch in Toowoomba. It was a special service where their pastor singled our family out even though he didn't know us, with some special encouragement and words of scripture that confirmed our current direction of study and that God would provide and that this would be a year of "Jubilee" where God would bring release to us in our circumstances. At this service there was also a guest musician who we received great encouragement from. For some reason I had quite a large amount of cash on me that I had reserved for bill payments and felt God telling me I needed to give this to the musician to support his amazing ministry. I gave him the money even though I had no idea how we would pay the bills. After this the amount of work I received seemed to just snowball with people asking me to teach their children music. Our friends said later that they felt that God was just blessing us because of our willingness to give funds to God that was more than we could afford for His work. This was amazing as they didn't know what we had given or that we had given more than we could afford.

I had other friends offer me the use of their Granny flat in Gatton to set up as a music studio to accommodate the influx of students I was receiving to teach music. This was another amazing provision, as our property was 20 minutes' drive out of town and now I could set up to teach in a place where people didn't have to travel far for their children to have music lessons. I also had students that I would teach in their homes as I travelled to and from University. I also approached the Lutheran school in Gatton and they were happy for me to teach there as well which gave me another full day's work. At this point the water supplies on the farm had dried up to the point where we had stopped growing crops. I still had to cart water up to our cattle though on the back of our truck as our dams were completely dry. While the tanks were filling I would study for my University courses.

About this time I received a call from the state Education department and they offered me contract work teaching "Instrumental Music" (teaching band instruments and conducting ensembles) which turned into a couple of days work a week. It was a busy time. I was studying at almost a full time load, teaching music to a number of private students as well as a bit of work keeping the farm running.

The rain eventually came and the creeks flowed. By this time I had so much teaching work that I didn't have much time for growing crops. The government drought subsidies had concluded but we still had a large property debt to service which was way beyond what my teaching income could meet. I had grown a bit of Lucerne hay and had borrowed machinery to bale it. The price for hay was very good and I managed to sell some unneeded machinery and purchase some very old hay making gear, namely a mower, rake and baler. It was amazing, but this old gear kept on working well the entire time we were to grow Lucerne hay. It literally worked on a wing and a prayer. While other farmer's newer gear would constantly need repair, my old gear kept on going with barely any maintenance costs and no major breakdowns. For the remainder of the time I was studying and farming, I only grew Lucerne for hay and a little bit of other fodder crops. By this time I had picked up more teaching work with the State Education Department and had teaching work 5 days a week, of which a couple of days were part days. These part days allowed me to catch up on a bit of farm work. I completed my music Degree in three and a half years which was pretty amazing with all of the farm work and teaching work which I had to do as well raising our young family.

Once I finished the music degree, I moved straight on to a post graduate diploma in teaching in order to become a registered teacher. I did this study at half load and completed it in 2 years. During this time I was also given special "Permission to Teach" so I could teach normal music classes in state schools as well as running Instrumental programs in a few small schools. The irony was that when I had to do a teaching internship to complete my post graduate qualifications, I basically did an unpaid stint in teaching the same classes which I was already doing but had been getting paid for.

So throughout the last 2 or so years of study, I was growing Lucerne hay to service our payments and supplement my teaching income. I look back at this time in amazement at how the hay making had worked out. Most work associated with producing hay can be done at night or early morning, so I fell into the routine of mowing either early in the mornings or after I came home from my teaching work. Virtually all baling is done at night when the moisture content of the hay was just right, so there were many nights spent baling hay. The amazing thing is that usually baling needs to be done really late in the night or very early morning as in dry weather it can take a long time for the dew to fall to get enough moisture in the hay so all the leaf doesn't crush up into powder and the hay become just stalks. I remember regularly praying that God would allow the hay to be ready to bale in time to be finished before midnight as I couldn't afford to be up all night or continually be getting up at night to check the moisture content as I couldn't afford to be tired during my teaching work. God honoured this and most times the hay was ready to bale early in the evening and I never had insufficient sleep to do my teaching work effectively. This was truly a miracle. The other amazing thing is that over these years we had almost no hay get wet by rain before it was ready to bale. Once a crop is mowed, any rain on it during the drying process spoils it. Not only did rain spoil the crop, but also extended the time frame of the process of trying to get it dried out and baled. Getting hay wet after it was mowed lowered the price of the hay (which depended on how much it was spoiled due to amount of rain it had had on it) but mostly created much more work and stress. It was a miracle that God provided for us by preventing our hay from being spoiled by rain. During this whole period of time we hardly had any cuttings of hay get spoiled by rain which was very unusual. We would watch the weather reports intensely then trust God to make the right decision about when to mow the hay, keeping in mind that it had to be fit in around my teaching work.

At this point I have to acknowledge the work that my mother put in to help us through this time. Unlike mowing and baling, raking the hay had to be done during the day at just the right time. Too wet and the hay wouldn't dry evenly and too dry and the leaf would crush and fall off which reduced the quality of the crop dramatically. So while I would mow and bale outside of school hours, my mum did nearly all of the raking during the day. She was such a blessing and I could never have produced hay without her help. Mum was meticulous in checking the hay and getting it raked at the right time. She was very skilled at it and knew just when to start raking and how many times it had to be raked. She would discern what was happening with the weather and would always have it ready to bale before the next lot of rain came through. She was truly part of Gods miracle in getting us through these years.

I had been teaching music with Education Queensland for 3 years and was due to receive permanent hours, but at the end of my third year the regional coordinator that looked after music teaching appointments, said that there were many staff transferring back to South East Qld and that myself and several other teachers would lose their positions. We were advised to apply for other teaching positions if any became available. I applied for a teaching position at a Christian College at the Gold Coast which was a higher level management position. My wife and I felt so strongly that this was where God wanted us to move. We were bewildered when I didn't get the position. We continued to pray and still felt that this was where God was leading us. One day during a lunch break when I was teaching at a High School in Gatton, I went into the store room and knelt down and prayed and had an overwhelming feeling that I would shortly receive a phone call about the teaching position at the Gold Coast. I barely left the store room when the phone rang. It was the college wanting me to come for another interview to discuss how they could structure the music program to suit my personal strengths and experience. They strongly felt that God was leading them to offer me the position. The principal said to me just months after starting at the College that it was obvious the God had led me to that job which was very encouraging.

While like every position, there were highlights and challenges over the 6 years I worked at this College. In my last 2 years at the Gold Coast College, it became increasingly apparent that there were problems within the College and this was also beginning to affect our church which was connected to the College. In my last year at the Gold Coast, our Senior Pastor asked me about taking up a vacant position in the Leadership team of the church. At first I thought no way but over the subsequent weeks I strongly felt God's leading to take up the position which was then confirmed at the church AGM. There were some difficult things to work through and also some encouragements at how God was working in people's lives.

I was prepared to be in a long drawn out process of working through issues at the Gold Coast College and the church. However, a good friend had moved to teach at a Christian College at Dalby (a town just West of Toowoomba in the Darling Downs), and encouraged me to apply for a music teaching position that had become available. We discounted it at first and thought it couldn't possibly be a good time to move. I applied for the job, just thinking it would be a beneficial experience to go through the application process. After being interviewed, I was offered the position and for some reason the opportunity to take this position just didn't seem to close and we felt more and more strongly that it was where God was leading us. I didn't see how we could organise a move in order to start teaching at the Dalby College at the beginning of this year and also not walk away from issues that needed to be dealt with at my current College and church. The principle so strongly believed that God was leading them to have me teach at the College at Dalby, that he offered for me to have an extra term at the Gold Coast to wrap things up. It just became more clearer that it was where God wanted us to move and that He would take care of the issues at the Coast. It has been amazing how God has led through the purchase of a home at Dalby and opened up the way to move there. As I sit and write this we have just started this next adventure and looking forward in anticipation how God will provide in this next step, particularly now with the world in Lockdown with the Covid 19 Coronavirus and churches closed for meetings. Also as I was finishing up at the Gold Coast College (where I had been working for over the last 6 years), they have already started putting off staff as enrolments drop as parents of students lose their jobs and can't afford to pay school fees. God is sovereign and will work His purposes out and build His Church through it all.

All praise and honour be to "Jehovah Jireh" God the provider!

25 THE BEST DAY OF MY LIFE

My name is Isabelle Dunlop, and I am the second oldest of seven children. I live in Laidley and have a passion for writing and expressing myself through art. I hope this testimony will inspire and spark a flame of faith in the hearts of readers.

"If I ride the wings of the morning, if I dwell by the farthest oceans, even there your hand will guide me, and your strength will support me." **Psalms 139:9-10.**

"Today was the best day of my life!" I smiled at everyone.

I remember announcing this at the dinner table when I was six years old. I remember, too, that Mum and Dad had stared at me as if I was one very confused child. Why? Earlier that evening, I had scared myself, and everyone, by almost drowning.

Dad asked me why I would say that today, of all days, was the best one of my life. I told him that it was because it was because God had saved me. That this was the best day because God had showed me that he had a reason for my life.

That morning, we had visited a friend's house. They had a small pool on their back veranda and a few of us had decided to cool off for a while. Mum sat on the side chatting to another parent, watching us play.

There was a sudden drop-off in the middle of the pool, and I crossed it.

One minute I was enjoying the cool water, the next I was struggling for air and my feet could no longer touch the bottom of the pool.

I was known for looking as if I were drowning when I played, so Mum had a hard time differentiating between the two. This time was different, she noticed the sporadic thrashing. My face began to turn white, and she realized I wasn't playing.

I've never seen Mum move that fast. She jumped into the pool like lightning, pulling me out of the water and lifting me onto the hard edge of the pool. I coughed up all the chlorine-water I had swallowed and found that I could breathe again. It's a nice feeling. Thanks Mum.

It was the best day of my life, because God had saved me for a greater purpose. Those were the words of six-year-old me.

When I was seven years old, I was diagnosed with pneumonia. Eventually, after about a week of laying in a hospital bed, Dad took me home. My condition could have become worse, but God saved me. Again.

When I was nine, I was baptized. I gave my life to Jesus Christ and left it at the foot of the cross.

John 3:16 tells us, "For God so loved the world that he gave his one and only Son, that whoever believes in him shall not perish but have eternal life."

Jesus gave his life for me, and I want to give my life for him. I want to serve him with all that I am, so that one day, I hope, I can hear him say,

"Well done, good and faithful servant."

Because my life isn't mine. I gave it to Jesus.

I am so, so far from perfect, and I need God's help badly. But he has promised his help and will guide us every step of the way.

26 ONE OF A KIND

Ron Neuendorf is the oldest member of Tenthill Baptist Church and first started attending, he says, in his mother's womb over 90 years ago. Ron and Joy, his wife of 65 years at the time of writing in 2022, testify to the faithfulness of God and answers to prayers in remarkable circumstances over their long and eventful lives. This story was written by Joy.

The day we learnt how to praise God, even in a time of drought started off like any other for this nearing 89 year old trusty, gutsy farmer on this June morning in 2019. He had set out to rake some newly mowed lucerne with his usual phone and spray for his angina in his pocket. About half way into completing his task he began to suffer chest pains. After administering the spray the pain did not subside so he decided to repeat the dose which he never should have done. However that is the last thing he remembered as his blood pressure went so low as to render him unconscious. How long for he has no idea. When he came to he found himself on the floor of the tractor wedged under the clutch. However he was able to free himself and get back on the seat with only minor injury. To his dismay the tractor had driven through a barbed wire fence, down into the usually full but now empty dam because of the drought, and half way up the other side before the engine stalled. So what did he do but drive the tractor back and finish his raking the hay before driving it back to the shed and walking back home.

As I, Joy, was recuperating after a knee operation, and as it happened daughter Lyndell and Ruth Peterson (nee Windolf) had come to clean house and do washing for me. So, thankfully I was not alone when the bedraggled human being stood at the doorway. On relating his story the girls quickly sprung into action and called triple O. So off to the hospital he unwillingly went. When he repeated his story to the nurse in charge she said, "What did you say you did when you came to?"

"I just got back on the seat and finished what I had set out to do," Ron remarked casually.

She shook her head and said, "Gee, they don't make them like that anymore."

Editor's note. When I took the image of Ron and Joy three years after the event, Ron was in his work shirt. You guessed it, he had been out on the tractor. Definitely, they don't make them like you now Ron. More's the pity.

27 GOD'S GRACE FOR HEALING

This testimony about the faithfulness of God in healing conditions that were medically impossible is told by Geoff Cooper. Geoff loves nothing more than to pray for the needs of anyone in the church and those who he comes across. Many more stories could be included but I will leave that for others to tell.

"All things *are* possible to him that believeth." Mark 9:23

It has been my experience through generations that when we stood on God's promises for healing that we have had wonderful results. It goes back to my uncle Harry who was blown up in a trench during World War One and apparently mortally wounded and given only days to live. He survived the initial encounter and throughout his life he was told by multiple doctors that he could not possibly live a lengthy life. But he stood on the promise that he would not die but live and that he would declare the works of God (Psm 118:17). He lived to the right old age of about 95 or 96 because of his belief in the promises of God.

In the 1940's I had a cousin diagnosed with Polio (before the vaccine was developed). Her mother was told by the doctors that her daughter had days to live and that there was no hope for her survival. Her mother didn't accept that and they took the girl's handkerchief into the church and prayed and claimed the healing promises over it. Now this woman is well into her 80's, completely healed and living a fruitful life.

I personally had a back condition which caused me severe pain for about 20 years. It also cost me a lot of money after multiple visits to doctors, chiropractors, physiotherapists, and acupuncture. Finally, I visited a top neurosurgeon who told me that I could not avoid having surgery. I elected not to have that surgery and put up with the discomfort. Eventually I met a born again Christian in the workplace and he informed me that in his church they emphatically believed in the healing power of Christ. I visited the church and it happened that there was a visiting pastor that had a wonderful anointing for healing. He laid hands on me, prayed over me the healing prayer of faith and I was instantly healed. That is almost 20 years ago and I have never had a back problem since.

In 2018 I was diagnosed with bladder and prostate cancer and had to go through surgery to have the prostate removed. The surgeons were concerned about the severity of the cancer and I stood on the promises of God and believed that "by his stripes we are healed." And God honoured that belief with his faithfulness and grace in his desire to heal.

28 GETTING OFF THE TIGHTROPE

*This is the account of Gracie **Harris/Hitila**'s journey of faith and was read to the church on the day of her baptism in May 2022. Gracie is the daughter of Heidi and step daughter of Nettal whose story of faith immediately precedes this.*

Good Morning everyone. For those you don't know or can't remember, my name is Gracie. I'm called that because at the time that I was born, it was only God's grace that could help me and my mother through the trial that we were facing and it is only because of God's grace that I can stand here sound minded and not as the traumatized small child I once was. I am clear minded and confident. Yes, sometimes it gets dark and I can't see, but it's not the darkness one feels when they are lost or trapped, for I am found.

My family have always been believers, I was raised going to church, singing, praying and worshiping, I was always God's child. But for me, even through that upbringing, life before this moment, before baptism and before this promise to Christ, is like walking a thin wire. It looks straight ahead, but it is deceiving. It wobbles and shakes and every time it does, there's the chance for you to fall. From that shake or wobble, you could fall on either side of the rope; to the believing side, or to the non-believing side.

Today I'm stepping off my wobbly rope. I know that my path will be full of turns, twists, obstacles and trials, but with trust in my Father, it will be firm.

I've been waiting to get baptized for quite a while, a little like the Jews in the desert or Esther and her banquets, waiting for the right moment, the right time. The night I decided that that was my path I had randomly opened my Bible and read Proverbs 3:3, *Let not love and faithfulness forsake you; bind them around your neck and write them on the tablet of your heart.* That night was the night I made a promise. I bound my Lord around my neck and wrote him on the tablet of my heart. I could no longer forsake him, he was in me and he was there wherever I went.

Some people ask, 'But how do you know he is real? How do you know that he is God?' And to that I can simply say, "You don't always do." There's a time, there's always a time in someone's life when they doubt, when the wire begins to wobble and shake, but without Christ there's a light that doesn't burn. Before that light is lit, you don't know, you can't see anything different, anything more or less real. But as soon as a spark, it doesn't matter the size, is put to that wick, then you know. You can see the reality, the difference and deep inside, every heart yearns for it.

As a small child I heard stories of my family hearing Jesus speak and I always wanted to experience that myself. Sometimes I'd lay in bed and imagine I did, but of course my imagination never gave me the spark I wanted. One night, I did hear the Lord speak. I was praying for rain in the large drought we had not long ago and he told me, "When your wine cup overflows and wets the land around, then so too shall mine." I was given the spark I needed and since then, I could see the reality and I knew my Father was there.

When someone knows why they do something, what standard they uphold and who they serve, they know who they are too. A life of believing brings love, reassurance and also confidence. When you are confident, confident in your day, confident in your life, confident in the face of death. When you are like that, there are no 'what if's' and there is no fear. That is what every believer on all of their separate journeys tries to accomplish, confidence. I am confident here today to take this step, make this promise. I am confident that my God is the one and only living god and that he died for me and was resurrected; and my confidence will grow throughout my life as a believer, just like every believer in Christ before me as we journey with God.

So baptism to me isn't just finding Christ, being reborn or suddenly believing for the first time, it's making a promise to the world and to the Lord that I am willing to follow wherever he goes and never forsake him. A life of faith, my life of faith isn't summed up with commandments or an order; those things are important and included in it, but for me the summing up comes from the simple statement the centurion in the Bible told Jesus. He said, *For I too am I man under authority and when my master says 'go!' I go; 'come' and I come.*

It doesn't matter what law, place, scenario, thing, person or decision I'm faced with, when the Lord says 'go', I will go. "Come' and I will come.

29 CALLED TO WALK TOGETHER

We're Mick and Megan Jones and together with our three kids Madison, Levi and Elora we moved to Laidley from the outskirts of Brisbane in December of 2017. We were looking for some wide open spaces and a change of scenery, both of which we have found in abundance here in the beautiful Lockyer Valley. We made our way out to Tenthill Baptist during a period of lockdown in 2020 which had most places still closed. We were greeted with warmth and hospitality and have loved fellowshipping there ever since.

"But God commendeth his love toward us, in that, while we were yet sinners, Christ died for us." Romans 5:8

The Lord has been so kind to us.

We see it as a huge mercy to us and to our children that we have been able to walk this road together.

My nana and my dad and probably others too, prayed for years that I would come to know Jesus after wandering off after my own desires as a teen. When Mick entered the picture they prayed for him too.

After about a decade of worldly living, during which time Mick and I got married and welcomed little Madison (Madi). I began to feel that I needed to know God and I wanted my new little family to know him too. I struggled a lot with bitterness and sadness that I had hung onto for a long time. I actually had no idea how to know God and I didn't really trust Christians. Through some dodgy experiences, I had come to the conclusion that Christians were only concerned with the appearance of things and not so much the living out of what they professed. It didn't cross my mind to open a Bible or even to talk to family (who are all believers).

Mick worked away week on-week off at the time. I was happy when he was home, but when he was gone it was just Madi and me at home and I had a lot of time alone with my thoughts. I started to have these experiences where I would wake up in the middle of the night and I couldn't move or speak. It was terrifying and it felt like something was holding me down. For several weeks this continued most nights and at one stage I thought, "If I can just say the name of Jesus, this will stop". I tried and even though I couldn't actually say the word, it stopped immediately. The next time it happened I did the same and it stopped again. I sat up in my bed and I prayed. A verse that I hadn't heard in a long time came to mind, "Come to me all you who are weary and heavy laden and I will give you rest" (Matt 11:28).

I surrendered to Jesus and I asked his forgiveness. I lay back down and went to sleep and I woke up a brand new person and I never had sleep paralysis again. I found my Bible, opened to the Gospel of John and I started reading. It blew my mind! As I read, everything fell into place and I could understand, finally, what Jesus had done for me and how I needed to respond. I started with all of the gospels, then started at Genesis, then the gospels again and the rest of the New Testament, I couldn't get enough. I was finally free and I was so happy about it, but Mick didn't know what had happened. I wanted to tell him straight away, but I was a little worried about what he might say.

Little did I know that the Lord had been working on his heart for a while too. He wasn't sure how to tell me! A year or so earlier he had come across a radio show in the early mornings on his way to work, I think it was Chuck Swindoll, and rather than changing the station and looking for something else to listen to (like he would have done in the past) he kept listening. Shortly afterwards, he met some Christians at work and started going to a Bible study out at camp; the chaplain out there gave him a Bible and some good material to listen to. A friend that Mick worked with shared about the Bible with him and his enthusiasm really got Mick curious.

He became especially interested to learn about Bible archeology and how many sites and items had been found that backed up the Bible narrative as historically true and having realised that the Bible was credible, he wanted to know what it had to say. He was convinced that it was true and he wanted to pursue the truth. He got saved too, within a short time of me, and we were off on a brand new adventure. I was baptised on Christmas day 2015 and Mick a few months later.

Life has been very different since then. We have witnessed God's love and kindness every step of the way as we are learning to pursue Jesus and to look to him in all things.

Thank you Lord for your goodness, faithfulness and steadfast love!

30 THE LORD STOPPED A BOLTING HORSE

Mary Russell grew up on a wheat and cattle property in Miles in country Queensland and knew the hectic pace of farm life and a country school. She married in 2006 and had six years of tender companionship before her husband died. Then after travelling for a year she realised that city life was not for her and she came to the Lockyer Valley to be near family.

"He the pearly gates will open, So that I may enter in; For He purchased my redemption And forgave me all my sin."

I was born the ninth child into a family of eleven siblings and had a strong Scottish and Welsh heritage. We lived in a farming community and our home life was built on the words of the Bible. This consisted of learning Bible verses by rote, having morning devotions, and on Sunday afternoons we had to read the Bible ourselves while we had a rest. However, I resisted this type of discipline and retaliated in any way that I could without getting into much trouble.

My escape from this was to ride my horse and just get away from the house. One Sunday when I was about eighteen and should have been meditating on scriptures, I saddled up my horse and rode towards the range in Toowoomba, but before I could get out of the the yard, I leaned over to open the gate and my horse was spooked and took off before the gate was properly opened. This left the horse with a piece of wood in his withers which caused him to buck. This in turn caused me to come off the horse except my foot was stuck in the stirrup! He bolted. My shirt was torn and I was covered in scratches and blood and it was at this time I realised that I could die while being dragged by my horse.

I then called out to God saying, "I don't want to die like this, please save me God." Just like that my horse slowed down to a walk at which time I was able to untangle my foot from the stirrup.

Once the horse stopped I asked God to forgive me and make me one of his own. Upon getting home my mother noticed I was upset and asked what was wrong. I asked her to forgive me as I felt I had been really defiant towards the Word of God. From that day I was more eager to listen to the daily devotions and read the Bible and I gave my life to the Lord. I still had bursts of temper but overall, my attitude had an amazing change.

31 A FRIEND OF MINE

I wanted to complete this book of testimonies with one from outside of those who have called Tenthill Baptist Church their home. I believe that every church where Christ is honoured can produce its own book of stories showing our heavenly father's loving care for his children. This testimony is from Dell Sippel (nee Guymer) who in 2005 had a very serious health crisis. Del, and her husband Wayne, were farmers in Tenthill and are members of Peace Lutheran Church in Gatton.

"My God stands beside me like a mighty warrior." I am not afraid. He is a friend of mine Jeremiah 20:11

I was born In Warwick on Good Friday 3rd April 1953. Christened in the Presbyterian Church of that year. It was during a Sunday School lesson taken by Miss Kirkegaard, an elderly teacher with her hair in an old-fashioned bun and, seated in front of a stained-glass window with the sun streaming in, that *my* life was changed. I was ten years of age. The lesson she delivered that morning was so powerful (although l cannot recall what it was about) that at that moment I felt something in my heart. I now realize what that was! I was confirmed in that Wesleyian Methodist Church in December 1966.

I completed my education at Warwick State High School following that our family transferred to Toowoomba. Unemployment was high and the opportunity to find Secretarial/Stenography work (being new to the district) was very challenging. Thankfully with excellent character references (plus report cards) in my hand I walked the pavements of Toowoomba looking for employment. Unbeknown to me there had been a vacancy for a Junior Secretary however interviews had been undertaken and had been narrowed down to three young ladies sitting for the final interview. Thankfully those interviewing said I deserved an interview also. I was employed that day. All prayers had been answered. I worked for three brothers, one of whom had presented me on my first day of High School with a Gideons Bible many years before

It was Christian workplace and the perfect place to strengthen Christian values of a teenager. Life was busy with work, youth group activities and Rural Youth dances It was on such a night at a Rural Youth dance I met Wayne from the Lockyer Valley who would, two years later, become my husband. Life changed again but a very different lifestyle awaited me, swapping shorthand for raking hay, grading onions, baling hay etc., and all that a horticultural farm entailed. It was very busy especially as we welcomed the arrival of our children Loren, Matthew Amy and Jonathan.

The children were educated and working or at University when in 2005 I was given the diagnosis of non-Hodgkin's lymphoma. Wayne and I faced this as we did all other trials in our life ....

together and in prayer. It was suggested we both go to Brisbane as I was given about 10% chance of survival and the treatment was gruelling and travel back and forth not the best option. The farm was in a drought cycle and therefore, on Doctors suggestion, it was easier to leave the farm .We were grateful for the help at that time of Mr. Sid Bichel, Nick Hall and Tim Schultz in mowing, chaffing and selling the small amount of lucerne remaining .This kept the accounts paid.

The treatment was harsh and during this time I was scheduled to have a very confronting test. I was in the theatre alone waiting for the medical practitioner and felt terrified. And then at that moment I felt a hand on my shoulder and a feeling of peace came over me. **There was no one in the room.** The treatment took its toll on my strength. I came home to Tent Hill nine months later in September 2006. The strength that we gained as a family and personally, from all the prayers coming from all Denominations in Gatton during this gruelling time can never be underestimated. It is indeed something to behold. My God was at work. I could feel the strength. My Oncologist was a genius and I was surrounded and cared for by many Nurses who were women of faith. Mr. Graham Huff from Lutheran Church of Australia visited every Thursday for nine months. Love parcels, letters and cards from the Valley were blessings indeed.

It was 15 years ago that we experienced this miracle. Miracles are still happening. We need to look for them! As a family we are truly blessed – Henry, Thomas, Jacob, Ned and Lewis, our delightful grandchildren have been born since our return from Brisbane.

We are so thankful.

"GREAT IS THY FAITHFULNESS LORD UNTO ME '

ABOUT THE EDITOR

Edgar Stubbersfield (known as Ted) grew up in the small town of Gatton in Queensland, Australia in the 50's. It was a good time to be young. Life was simple, relatively safe and faith in God was taken for granted. After being thrown out of school in 1965 he started an apprenticeship as a motor mechanic, something he was ill suited to. In 1970, Ted went on an extended trip overseas and was confronted by the Christian gospel in many countries and saw for the first time that there was a God who was alive. That year he met with Jesus in a Damascus road type experience.

Ministry seemed to be the logical call on his life and he trained initially with the Church of Christ and then in the UK with the Elim Pentecostal Church but found himself most at home with a remarkable group of Grace Baptists. The Lord had mercy on His church and Ted went back to the family business, a sawmill. He kept his interest in Christian faith, living and doctrine by studying by correspondence and by writing. He completed a Master of Theology in Applied Theology in 2011 through the University of Wales.

Ted has a number of other publications but in a very different field, weather exposed timber structures. He is currently working as a consultant in this field.

www.ingramcontent.com/pod-product-compliance
Lightning Source LLC
Chambersburg PA
CBHW061734020426
42331CB00006B/1240